# Barcelona:
# The Civic Stage

*A PORTRAIT IN URBAN CIVILIZATION*

# Barcelona:
# The Civic Stage

By Robert Goldston

Illustrated by Donald Carrick

The Macmillan Company
Collier-Macmillan Limited, London

*FOR CHRISTAL WALKER*
*and*
*ERIK and SOLVEIG GYLLENSVÄRD*

# Contents

# Fifth Row Center

*Oh! Happy the city with a mountain beside it,*
*for it can admire itself from on high.*

— JUAN MARAGALL

And the citizens of Barcelona have been doing just that for more than two thousand years with considerable justification. For there is a lot to admire in this big, bustling, brilliant theater-by-the-sea. Take the stage itself, for example—a broad (but not too broad) plain surrounded by imposing (but not overbearing) hills, embraced by the deep, warm blue of the Mediterranean and lit by the lighter blue of normally cloudless skies. In front of the stage is an orchestra pit, Barcelona harbor, 305 acres of still water protected by two giant concrete arms in which a philharmonic of whistles, horns, hammers, riveters, chugging engines and creaking cranes is constantly tuning up for some iron-voiced industrial symphony. And though the stage is bounded and defined by the hills of Tibidabo and Montjuich and the small rivers Llobregat and Besós on either side, it has no rear—it is an open stage leading into the province of Catalonia and, beyond, into Spain. There is no finer natural theater anywhere in the world in which to stage the urban drama.

Nor are there many cities which can boast of a greater variety and collection of sets and properties. There is a beautifully preserved Gothic Quarter dominated by an ancient cathedral and Renaissance palaces, laced by narrow, quiet streets and passageways in which a stroller can imagine himself part of a medieval morality play. There is a Chinese Quarter (which has nothing to do with the Far East), a hodgepodge of tattered buildings, cheap hotels, garish dance halls, neon-streaked night clubs, cafés and restaurants in which a stroller can imagine himself part of a continuing immorality play. There is the great central artery of the Ramblas (literally, "place to stroll, ramble"), a series of very broad avenues bisected by pedestrian malls on which thousands of citizens parade slowly back and forth, importuned by kiosks at which they can buy brilliantly colored flowers, even more brilliantly colored birds, newspapers and books, hot snacks or the outdoor café tables from which thousands of other citizens are watching the parade. There are the solid square miles of stately nineteenth century houses in which people can lead, if they wish, Victorian lives; the outer districts of brightly colored and brilliantly designed concrete and glass apartment houses in which people can, if they wish, lead modern lives; the appallingly filthy-appearing and congested tumble-down slums north and south of the harbor in which people have a hard time leading any kind of life at all.

And there are the stage properties—more diversified and diverting than can be found in most cities. There are nineteenth century exhibition palaces that look like wedding cakes designed by oriental chefs; exotically beautiful parks ranging from the subtropical formality of Ciudadela to the surrealistic fantasy of Parque Guëll; the startling buildings designed by the great Catalan architect Antoni Gaudí i Cornet (apartment and office buildings that look like practical jokes, a still incomplete cathedral that looks like Faith, in frozen lava) dotting the city; great plazas decorated with fantastic fountains and girdled by thousands of desperate motorists trying to escape circular traffic jams; a vast amusement park on the slopes of Montjuich in which roller-coasting citizens can get upside-down views of the city below; satisfactorily grim fortresses; the Pueblo Español (a Hispanic Disneyland of architectural styles, costumes and folklore from all over Spain); some of the world's most important museums; several soccer fields in which 150,000 fans shout themselves hoarse every weekend; two bullrings in which 55,000 *aficionados* jeer or cheer an ancient and symbolic ritual every Sunday; hundreds of churches in which worshipers celebrate another ancient and symbolic ritual every Sunday; and, of course, thousands of outdoor cafés at which people can gather to discuss all this.

And then there are the actors themselves, about 1,500,000 citizens of Barcelona, very proud of their theater, very conscious of their roles. They are the inheritors and shapers of three great cultures; the na-

3   *Fifth Row Center*

*Mediterranean harbor—the view from Montjuich. Columbus points westward from atop his column at the foot of the Ramblas while sightseers travel over the harbor by cable car.*

tional, official and most apparent Spanish culture; the more circumscribed but very rich Catalan culture; and a self-assumed and well-justified international, cosmopolitan culture based on trade, tourism and history. In order of loyalties, the average citizen of Barcelona would probably place his city first, Catalonia second, the world third and Spain last. If this mixture of cultures and conflict of loyalties has given the city a stormy history, it has also given its life a colorful variety and a more concentrated sense of civic spirit. Because of a carefully cultivated sense of apartness on the part of Catalans, and the opposition or repression it has often evoked from official Spain, Catalan men of ability and ambition have often found their outlet in provincial and civic leadership—with great benefits to Catalonia and Barcelona. And cultural connections with France (just a hundred miles north) and the outer world have given Barcelona a more cosmopolitan and urbane character (expressed not only in the manners of citizens but also in buildings) than is to be found in the rest of urban Spain.

But too much should not be made of the differences between the people of Barcelona and those, say, of Madrid. The citizens of both cities display traditional Spanish characteristics of courtesy, pride, vivacity and wit. It is perhaps true that the Catalan is something more of a businessman, perhaps a bit more energetic, more aggressive than the Castilian—but this appears to be due much more to social and economic history than to any ethnic factor. Of greater interest still is the conflict between the Spanish and the Catalan tempers, existing within the same people, insofar as it produces the tension basic to the urban drama of Barcelona. The

Spaniard, for reasons of a very real and calculable kind,* has long viewed himself as an actor on the stage of history. The Spanish language, though derived from the same Latin sources as French and Italian, has become over the centuries much more declamatory than either. It is, in fact, as much an ethic as a language, its words weighted with moral and dramatic significance, its construction lending itself most aptly to self-dramatization. The Spanish temper is a noble but brittle shell, a role within which lives an individual who is rarely able to distinguish his personal from his public character. This leads to all sorts of paradoxes but lends a dignity and nobility to Spanish life that has disappeared elsewhere. On the other hand, the Catalan temperament, its sources drawing from the diverse world of Mediterranean commerce, from the blood and historical relationship of its culture to that of southern France, and from an industrial heritage common to all western Europe, is recognizably modern. But for the heavy influence of Spain in Catalonia and Barcelona, the citizens of these regions would not be very different from those of Marseilles, Genoa or Milan. But the pervasiveness of the Spanish temper, with its emphasis on role playing, combined with the historical factors which have concentrated Catalan attention upon local affairs, produces in Barcelona an intense sense of life as an urban drama in which each citizen has his part. This in turn shapes and defines an urban way of life based on civic consciousness—a way of life of a congeniality, satisfaction and inner order which is to be

* For a discussion regarding the Spanish temper and its sources, readers are referred to the author's *Spain* (Macmillan, 1967) and *The Civil War in Spain* (Bobbs-Merrill, 1967).

*Proud emblems of civic independence are hidden in the very old walls of ancient buildings.*

found in practically none of the world's other large cities.

For the city itself—the idea of a city, any city—is not merely a collection of buildings, however imposing, nor a massing of people, however many. The city has always been a shrine to which men flocked to worship —to worship the gods or God or themselves in their highest expressions of culture. It is a place where people, much more isolated *personally* than in a town or village, consciously identify themselves with public symbols, with their fellow men on a more impersonal scale. It is the place where, hopefully, a better-than-personal character can be formed by the self-conscious performance of a public role, where the availability of higher expressions of art, law and government provide a means for rationalizing existence and informing it with more than the merely private, the merely necessary. When a city fulfills this function its citizens are said to be seized of civic pride, civic responsibility, even civic virtue. Thus the city was, in one of its deepest senses, always meant to be a stage upon which people could perform. Its streets and avenues, its buildings and monuments, its customs and government were all meant to provide a scope for drama—not only the drama of conventional ceremonies but also the daily drama of people living together with a sense of mission. But this mission must be both personally ennobling and capable of collective rather than simply individual expression. Where a former sense of mission has been destroyed (as in London or Paris or Boston), cities are in the process of decay and, perhaps, eventual disappearance as urbane places to live. Where the sense of mission has been perverted to mere self-aggrandizement (as in New York or San Francisco) the city becomes an urban jungle, a chaotic wasteland of personal greed and public disorder. Nor can the imposition from above of outdated superhuman "missions," such as the advancement of the power of the state (as in Moscow or Washington), bring anything but eventual ruin to the citizens of such cities (as the fate of Berlin, Tokyo and a dozen other capitals in the past fifty years testifies) while surrounding them with urban wastelands of impersonal monuments to private or collective power.

Since the decay of the ages of faith (and the end of the secure medieval civic order whose monuments still delight, inspire and ennoble the citizens of those cities fortunate enough to have them), the only satisfactory objects of worship at the civic shrine have been humanity and life itself. The only secure and ennobling mission of the people of cities has been the advancement of those arts and sciences (and their communication to the rest of the world) which are the highest expressions of human culture and which, hopefully, may one day produce a truly mature, truly humane worldwide civilization.

It may be asked, "But do people, individually or collectively, really consciously *perform*, aware of their participation in an urban drama, aware of any sort of mission?" No, of course not. There may be a few who perceive themselves in such roles. But even in Barcelona, with its special emphasis on drama, very few people indeed are aware of the implications of the way they live. For the urban drama is expressed primarily as a *way of life*—a way of life in detail, and people are not normally self-conscious about the way they live. Yet to an observer (especially one from America, where urban drama is all but unknown and a sense of civic mission only a dim memory), there is no doubt that Barcelona is an unself-consciously created theater in which a most vivid human drama continues to be performed.

This would seem to argue the continuance of a sense of mission among its citizens—conscious or otherwise. And no visitor to Barcelona can doubt that its urbanity, its civic pride, is still informed by the mission of furthering human culture and art—of creating a humane way of life. It is one of the last (and probably the largest) cities on earth of which this can still be said, and for very definite historic reasons.

Barcelona, like other Spanish cities, is coming late into the modern world. Although in certain physical respects it once led the way (its electric light system, public gas system and telephone exchange were among

*Painters, street sweepers—no strangers to each other on the Ramblas.*

the world's first), various national and international factors over which the citizens of Barcelona had no control combined to stop the clock of history, or at least to slow it down, for nearly sixty years—a long time in today's hurried world. For the past ten years that clock has been ticking again in Catalonia and throughout Spain. Progress has been telescoped dramatically, until today Barcelona is once again approaching the front rank of urban modernity. Indeed, its new architecture, both residential and commercial, is more exciting than the new architecture to be found almost anywhere else, save perhaps Mexico City. But because human customs and ways of life change much more slowly than physical environment, the sense of mission in Barcelona has not yet been significantly eroded. Its people are still heavily committed to civic order, civic pride, civic responsibility. They still delight in a traditional urban drama.

Can these invaluable human factors survive the impact of modernity? On the physical level can the city avoid such traps as traffic strangulation; suicidal air pollution; the creation (through indifference and greed) of new, formalized public-housing slums to replace older individual slums; the eventual flight of its inhabitants to the suburbs and beyond, which spells the end of urbanity itself? This kind of physical decay has seemed to be the concomitant of progress in practically every other large city in the world. More importantly, can the citizens of Barcelona maintain their way of life in the face of the assaults beneath which the urban drama, civic pride and humane civilization have vanished from other cities? Is Barcelona's sense of humanistic mission doomed to be converted into the worship of naked power? Will its sense of civic responsibility be swamped by the tidal waves of personal greed? Will its urban drama be fragmented by individualistic chaos? All these antihuman impositions have been, apparently, the heavy price citizens of other cities have paid for presumed materialistic progress. That price has not yet been exacted from the people of Barcelona—but it may be soon. And if urbanity, civicism and a humane way of life cannot be maintained in Barcelona, it is very unlikely that they can be maintained anywhere on earth. And if that is true, then modern civilization would seem to be doomed to follow older civilizations which lost their human content, into the dustbin of history.

But not quite yet. Not so long as one city—Barcelona, in this case—can demonstrate to the world that modern civilization is compatible with humane existence. The way of life of the people of Barcelona is still today one which the citizens of other cities may truly envy, and one from which they have very much to learn. Meantime, unself-consciously or otherwise, the delightful, human urban drama continues in this city-theater. The stage décor changes slowly over the decades and centuries, the actors change more rapidly; but there is never an intermission in the show.

# 1 Barca, Barcino, Barcelona

*Abode of the rich, pleasant is Barcelona;*
*There a port opens its amorous arms;*
*The land bubbles always with sweet waters.*

—LORENZO RIBER

It was probably the sweet waters that proved irresistible to the earliest settlers of Barcelona. Coming perhaps from the arid interior of the Iberian peninsula, the sight of the rivers Llobregat and Besós tumbling down gentle foothills to the sea must have suggested to prehistoric men a site for settlement. Two nearby hills (present-day Montjuich and Tibidabo) would have afforded protection; the rivers would have provided not only water but transport into the interior; and of course the sea offered fish. Since Neolithic men seldom ventured more than a few hundred yards from shore, they would not have regarded Barcelona as a port. Yet the great bay between the Llobregat and the Besós recommended itself to seafaring men from the east.

There is no absolute proof that the Phoenicians established a settlement at Barcelona. But it is highly probable. Those keen merchant-adventurers from the shores of Palestine who established trading centers up and down the Iberian coast would hardly have overlooked Barcelona. It is probable that they established a trading center–settlement on the hill of Montjuich. And if that is true, then Phoenician Barcelona was also under the protection of the Phoenician gods—a shrine as well as a commercial center. To the ignorant Iberian tribes who came to trade with the Phoenicians, the skills of these highly civilized people would have appeared magical—and would have been ascribed to supernatural powers. In any event, the interior tribes never attacked the trading post, either in legend or later written history, which would argue strongly that it was regarded with traditional awe and reverence from earliest times.

The best evidence that the Phoenicians established a commercial-religious center at Barcelona is the fact that their direct heirs, the Carthaginians, certainly did. The Phoenician colony of Carthage, on the North African coast, waxing strong as Phoenicia itself declined, settled and conquered sites all along the Iberian coast (and into the interior). The name "Barcelona" was probably derived from that of the famous ruling family of Carthage, the Barcas. It is likely that Hamilcar Barca and his son Hannibal (said to have been born on the nearby island of Ibiza) named the Carthaginian settlement in honor of themselves: Barca, hence, Barcelona. When Hannibal crossed the Alps to attack Rome, his army included stone-slingers recruited from the Barcelona area.

*The fishermen's boats clustered in the harbor reflect nautical design going back to Phoenician times.*

The long and bitter wars between Carthage and Rome ended with the destruction of Carthage and brought Roman rule to the Iberian peninsula. The great Roman soldier-statesman Cato the Elder led Roman legions to Iberia in 201 B.C. and, after driving out the Carthaginians, established his veteran soldiers in colonies there, of which Barcelona was one. The rough Latin spoken by these soldiers, removed in space and, slowly, in time, from Roman Latin, supposedly developed into Catalan (Cato's Latin). The Roman colony called itself Barcino and was built, not on the Carthaginian site of Montjuich, but on the hill the Romans called Taber—site of the present-day Gothic Quarter.

Roman Barcino (its full name was the staggering Colonia Faventia Julia Augusta Paterna Barcino) was laid out and organized on the same plan used by the Romans for practically all their settlements—rigorously four-square with a gridiron pattern of streets. It was equipped with a forum, public baths, an arena and a citadel. Its citizens enjoyed such standard Roman amenities as central heating, well-paved roads, bathrooms and toilets, and both private and public lighting systems (using oil). But during the first and second centuries A.D. Barcelona was evidently a very provincial place. Pomponia Mela, writing of Paterna Barcino at that time, complained that the city "lacked happenings." Yet there is evidence that the commercial spirit first instilled by the Phoenicians and Carthaginians still ruled Roman Barcino. It was a busy port and the inland tribes continued to bring their wares there to trade.

If Barcino lacked happenings, it also lacked a wall.

That was not uncommon among Roman towns for the Romans felt that the great size and efficiency of their armies were guarantee enough against potential aggression. But by the end of the third century A.D. Rome's armed might had dwindled to the point where Frankish and Germanic tribes, pouring down over the Pyrenees, were able to capture, sack and burn Paterna Barcino so that almost nothing of the city remained. Roman legions, summoned from the south, quickly drove off the northern invaders—but a pattern of aggression from beyond the Pyrenees had made its fatal appearance.

Paterna Barcino was rebuilt—this time with a fabulously high and thick wall encircling it. But the new Barcino was constructed not so much under the aegis of Roman power as under the sign of Christianity, which by that time had become the state religion of the Roman Empire. The city's continuing importance is argued by the construction of a very large basilica within the new walls. Nor was its history forgotten; the Roman poet Ausonius wrote during the fourth century to St. Paul of Nola that he had prayed in the basilica of "Punic Barcino" (Carthaginian Barcino).

The second Roman Barcino was destined to be short-lived. Like other Roman cities, it suffered from the empire-wide economic crisis which, along with barbarian invasions, brought the ancient world to disaster. When the Visigoths again descended over the Pyrenees from present-day France in 415 A.D., they had little difficulty in capturing Barcino. The Visigothic king Ataulphus (married to Galla Placidia, daughter of the Roman Emperor Theodosius) established himself as monarch of an area roughly corresponding to modern Catalonia and made Barcino his capital. His choice of a capital city would seem to indicate not only the physical size and commercial importance of Barcino, but a continuing tradition of reverence for the place, inherited perhaps from Phoenician times.

It would be a mistake to assume that Barcino (called now variously Barcinona or Varcinona) fell into a sort of dark, semicivilized condition under the Visigoths. Despite the fact that the citizens of Barcelona found themselves pressed into service in the continuous wars waged by the petty Visigothic kings of Iberia, the Visigoths themselves were both Christian and fairly civilized. Furthermore, both they and their culture merged quickly into the Roman culture of their new subjects. It was not the Visigothic conquest that brought ruin to Iberia, but the Moorish.

Early in the eighth century A.D. a fierce tribe of North African warriors, the Moors, inflamed with fanatical zeal for Mohammed's teachings (and greed for the fields and mines of Iberia), conquered most of the Iberian peninsula in a swift *jehad* (holy war). When the Moors reached Barcelona, the city was in the throes of civil strife between the supporters of its Visigothic king, Rodrigo, and his opponents. A Moorish general, Abd-al-Aziz, taking shrewd advantage of the situation, offered his forces to help Rodrigo's enemies. Thus, in 717 A.D., the Moors entered Barcelona without a fight—as allies of some of the citizens. But, of course, they showed no disposition to leave. And after Rodrigo had fled, they simply took over the administration of the city. In return for this remarkably easy conquest, the Moors permitted the inhabitants of Barcelona to retain their personal and religious liberty unmolested

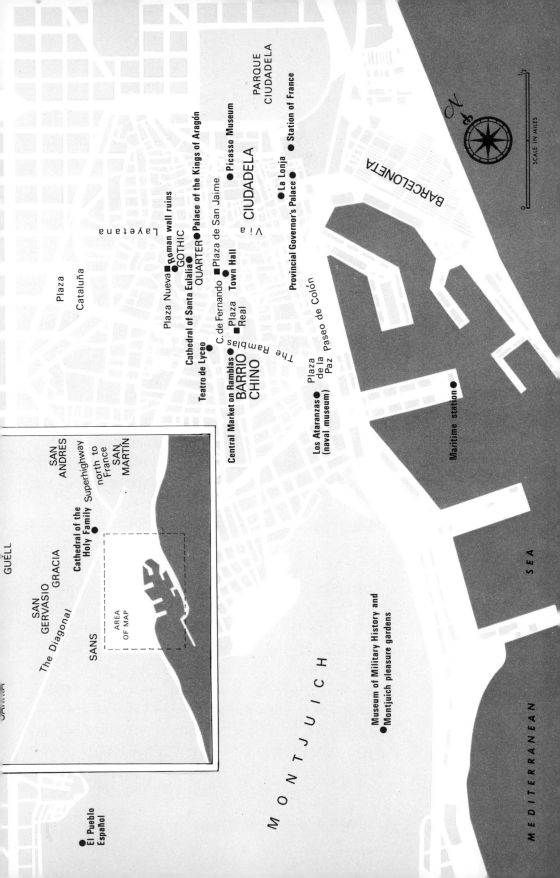

SAN ANDRES

SAN MARTÍN

GUELL

SAN GERVASIO GRACIA

The Diagonal

SANS

Cathedral of the Holy Family

Superhighway north to France

AREA OF MAP

El Pueblo Español

Plaza Cataluña

Layetana

Plaza Nueva ■ Roman wall ruins
GOTHIC
Cathedral of Santa Eulalia ● QUARTER ● Palace of the Kings of Aragón
Plaza de San Jaime
C. de Fernando ■ Town Hall
Teatro de Lyceo
Plaza ● CIUDADELA
Real
Central Market on Ramblas ●
BARRIO
CHINO
Plaza
de la
Paz

Los Atarazanas ●
(naval museum)

Picasso Museum ●

PARQUE CIUDADELA

Via ● La Lonja ● Station of France

Provincial Governor's Palace ●

Paseo de Colón

MONTJUICH

Museum of Military History and
Montjuich pleasure gardens ●

BARCELONETA

Maritime station ●

SEA

MEDITERRANEAN

N

SCALE IN MILES

0      ½

—and even established various Visigothic counts as puppet rulers of the region. But by 755 A.D. the Moorish power throughout Spain had grown so great that they no longer felt obliged to appease their subjects. The people of Barcelona found themselves slaves in their own city. The old Roman and Visigothic laws were replaced by Moorish tyranny; commerce and trade were heavily taxed, and, of greatest importance during those centuries of religious faith, Christianity was replaced by Mohammedanism as the official state religion. The citizens of Barcelona, who had encouraged the Moors to enter their city, were now faced with a bloody struggle to expel them.

But it was not the citizenry of Barcelona who drove out the Moors, but the armies of the great Frankish Emperor Charlemagne. With his own religious duties, political ambitions and dynastic pretensions in mind, Charlemagne invaded northern Spain to fight the Moors in 778 A.D. and again in 785 A.D. He was able to establish a protectorate over much of what is today Catalonia, called then the "Spanish Marches." And, in 813 A.D. Charlemagne's son, Louis the Pious, in cooperation with the citizens of Barcelona, finally drove the Moors from the city (they were to return with fire and sword very briefly in 985 A.D. under the leadership of Almanzor, once again to be quickly driven off by Franco-Catalan forces). So the Moors ruled Barcelona for barely a century, a fact of vital importance when it is realized that the rest of Spain had to fight for over seven hundred years to drive out the invaders. Those elements of the Spanish temper traceable to this age-long war of reconquest (soldierly virtues, fatalism in the face of death, fiery fanaticism, religious intolerance) did not develop among Catalans, but a dependence upon and cultural merging with Frankish influences did. In spite of the fact that the Catalan counts who ruled Catalonia as puppets of the Frankish descendants of Louis the Pious became increasingly independent over the centuries, the commercial and cultural ties of Frankish domination were never completely severed.

The Catalan language, which contains elements of Spanish, French and even Italian, is distinct from any of those tongues. But it is very close to a vanished language known as *langue d'oc* (literally, and charmingly, "language of yes"), once spoken throughout southern France. It was the speech of the semi-independent principalities of Provence and was part of a culture very different from that, say, of Paris. Provence was a land of poetry, gaiety, of troubadors and a cosmopolitan outlook born of Mediterranean commerce. It was also a land of reform-minded clergy and liberal feudal counts and princes. But at the beginning of the thirteenth century, the "heretical" nature of Provençal life had become such a thorn in the side of the Church in Rome that a great crusade was organized against the region—a crusade which killed a great number of the inhabitants and left southern France in chaos. Provence and its culture were almost completely wiped out, leaving Barcelona and Catalonia as isolated remnants. To this day Catalans occasionally wistfully refer to their land as "the country of *Gay Saber*," which means "the country of the poetry of langue d'oc."

Barcelona's rise to greatness as a port city did not, however, depend on its cultural ties with Provence. It

was based on its strategic situation as the commercial and shipping center between Moorish Africa (and southern Spain) and northern Europe (especially France). As French domination faded and the Moorish power in southern Spain declined, Barcelona and Catalonia prospered and the port city entered upon an age of Gothic splendor.

Barcelona's emergence as one of the world's great cities may conveniently be dated from 1058 A.D. It was in that year that Count Ramón Berenguer (first of a long line of independent and powerful Catalan counts) inaugurated a new cathedral (to replace the old basilica destroyed in Almanzor's raid of 985). The count took the occasion to confirm to the citizens their ancient rights and privileges in a code known as the "Usatges" (literally, "usages"). These included the right of general assembly of all citizens to approve laws; the right of citizens to be tried in their own Barcelona courts for certain crimes; the establishment of the office of mayor and, of great importance, the establishment of a council of important citizens to advise the mayor. Under Ramón Berenguer's successors these rights and privileges would sometimes be expanded, sometimes contracted—but they lasted over the centuries.

The slow but steady establishment of self-rule for the citizens of Barcelona reflected a process common to great trading cities during the Middle Ages. As a

*Berenguer the Great, mounted above an ancient Roman cemetery outside the northern walls of the Gothic Quarter. Above the royal palace rise the spires of the Cathedral of Santa Eulalia.*

money economy replaced a barter economy, the counts of Catalonia were in ever-increasing need of money to pay for their pleasures and for mercenary armies. This money could only be obtained through taxes, which depended upon the increasing wealth and commerce of Barcelona. In return for increased taxes, the citizens of Barcelona wrung ever greater rights and freedoms from the counts. As the only great urban center within Catalonia, Barcelona became almost a city-state.

The growth of Gothic Barcelona was slow but splendid. Very many of the medieval buildings are still standing and still in use. The churches and palaces erected during the thirteenth and fourteenth centuries show a mixture of architectural styles which reflects the city's cosmopolitan role during those centuries. There is the northern Gothic influence with its slim spires and vertical lines, its great vaulted rooms and flying buttresses. It is mixed with an older Greco-Roman classicism distinguished by pillars and horizontal lines—and decorated with bright frescoes and colored tiles in the Moorish manner. The new building reflected, too, a changing social scene. The cathedral (completed in 1298 and consecrated to St. Eulalia, patron saint of the city) was near splendid new palaces which housed the court of the counts of Catalonia. And not far away, during the fourteenth and fifteenth centuries, a town hall and a provincial palace were erected to house an ever-expanding and ever-more-powerful municipal administration. The city itself had

*The Town Hall on Plaza San Jaime—even the pavement is integrated into an artistic whole.*

long since expanded beyond the old Roman walls; a new wall had been built in the thirteenth century, incorporating much more land than the original, yet another wall was built during the fourteenth century, still more expansive. But it seemed that the wall builders could not keep pace with the city's growth, for they continued to enlarge their works all through the fifteenth, sixteenth and seventeenth centuries.

In 1137 A.D. Count Ramón Berenguer IV married Petronilla, queen of Aragón, and Barcelona became capital not only of Catalonia but also of the kingdom of Aragón. If the weight of royal power within the city was increased by its territorial expansion, so were the rights and opportunities of the citizens. Aragón laid claim, with increasing success, to lands and cities beyond the sea. The islands of Sardinia and Sicily, the city of Naples and many a commercial enclave between and beyond were to fall into the hands of the rulers of Aragón-Catalonia until, by the beginning of the sixteenth century, the Mediterranean began to look like a Catalan lake. All of which swelled the purses of Barcelona merchants. And with increasing commerce and wealth, municipal rights grew. The kings of Aragón ruled the city through deputies whose headquarters were the provincial palace, known as the Diputación. But across the square from the Diputación stood the town hall, where the mayor and the leading citizens of Barcelona exercised a power which was always expanding at the expense of the king's deputy. During the thirteenth century the council of important citizens who advised the mayor was increased to one hundred members. Despite the fact that this number increased or decreased over subsequent centuries it was ever after known as the Council of One Hundred.

The Council of One Hundred had the right to appoint six of its members as councillors to form a sort of cabinet for the mayor. From the very beginning this system encompassed a two-way power struggle. First, the Council of One Hundred constantly sought to increase its power at the expense of both the king's deputy and even the mayor; second, various classes of citizens of Barcelona used the council as an arena to struggle for power among themselves. Generally speaking, the inhabitants of Barcelona comprised three classes: citizens (including the aristocracy and the wealthiest people), merchants (whose strength increased steadily and from whose ranks new "citizens" would occasionally be drawn) and artisans, comprising the bulk of the population. During the middle of the fourteenth century the special group of six councillors comprised two citizens, two merchants and two artisans, a basic compromise which accurately reflected the relative power of the three groups.

The social structure of medieval Barcelona was dominated by the growth of guilds. As trade expanded and commercial life became more complex, the workers in a particular trade or craft, such as the fish-sellers or the goldsmiths or the carpenters, who usually lived close to one another (on streets which still today bear the names of their professions), would band together for mutual help and protection. But the guild was not a trade union. It was more like a clan, a great commercial family. The guild provided support for sick or disabled members, enforced rules of workmanship, set prices, offered prayers for the souls of departed workers and, above all, made sure that no one not a member of the guild practiced its particular trade or craft. Guild members were organized into three classes: the masters, who were richest and owned their own shops and employed others; journeymen, who often owned their own tools but were generally employed by masters; and apprentices, who owned nothing, knew nothing of the craft and lived at the whim and bounty of the master from whom they learned. Apprentices and journeymen had to spend specified numbers of years in their respective conditions before they were eligible for election to the rank of master.

The impulse to commercial expansion provided by Barcelona's location between Europe and Africa and its union with the Crown of Aragón was given powerful stimulus by its contacts with the Moors and, through them, with the world of Arabian scholarship. The Mohammedan civilization of southern Spain was Europe's greatest during medieval times. And the arts of mathematics and navigation, far advanced in the realms of Islam, were brought to Barcelona by the Jews who, unlike Catholics, were able to study at Mohammedan universities. The skills and sciences they brought to Barcelona placed the city far ahead of its commercial rivals. For example, marine insurance was invented in Barcelona, the first code of maritime law was established there in the thirteenth century (administered and enforced by the Consulado del Mar under joint royal and municipal authority) and Europe's first public bank, the Taula del Cambi, was opened in Barcelona in 1401.

The greatness achieved by Barcelona during the fourteenth and fifteenth centuries was the greatness possible to a city-state. True, Barcelona enjoyed the

benefits of exploiting the overseas colonies and connections of the crown of Aragón, and it did draw sus-
tenance from its Catalonian hinterland. But without
either Catalonia or Aragón, Barcelona would still have
achieved greatness. It did this almost solely as a port
city and commercial center. No wonder its citizens felt
fully self-sufficient and no wonder they opposed the
submergence of their city into larger political forms.

But by the end of the fifteenth century a more
complex, interdependent money economy had fully replaced barter; larger political units, nations, were coming into their own; and a resurgence of the zeal of
Islam (in the form of the arrival of the Turks in the
Middle East) had cut off trade with Asia. Like other
semi-independent cities in Europe, Barcelona could not
maintain its independence in the face of these factors.
In Spain itself, the long-drawn-out agony of the reconquest came to an end. In 1492 Ferdinand and Isabella
accepted the surrender of Granada, last Moorish
stronghold in Spain, and united the entire Iberian
peninsula, including Aragón and Barcelona, beneath
their rule. At the same time they dispatched Chris-
topher Columbus on his voyage over the Ocean Sea—
thereby signalizing the opening of new trade routes to
the east as well as the west. These twin events—the
establishment of a strong, central national power in
Spain and the end of Barcelona's trade hegemony—
marked the beginning of a slow but steady decline of
the city's power, freedoms and glory. In fact, all subsequent Barcelona history may be seen as an attempt
by the citizens of the city (and the province beyond)
to break away from centralized rule in order to once
again reach the levels of prosperity and grandeur

*The waterfront—Columbus again in the foreground (and a replica of his Santa Maria tied up nearby), dominating the Paseo de Colon. Note that some elements, at least, of the harbor are in immediate use by the people of the city.*

achieved during the early Renaissance centuries.

The accession through marriage of the Hapsburg monarchs to the Spanish throne at the beginning of the sixteenth century united Spain with Hapsburg domains in Holland, Belgium, Italy and Austria. Thus, when Charles I of Spain was elected Holy Roman Emperor (as Charles V of that empire), Spain found itself the strongest power in Europe and the center of a vast new overseas empire in the Americas. As Spain's principal shipbuilding center, Barcelona prospered. But like cities throughout the peninsula, it began to see an increasing proportion of its wealth siphoned off into imperial adventures, its boldest spirits drawn off to discoveries and settlements in the New World, its young men enlisted in the armies of the king-emperor on endless campaigns of conquest in Europe. The age of Spain's imperial dominion brought ruin to the country—in the form of inflation, depopulation and demoralization. All these factors were felt keenly in Barcelona, which, with its non-Spanish cultural heritage, felt itself being exploited by the central power in Madrid.

The Usatges, the rights and privileges of Barcelona, were reflected throughout Catalonia by the ancient rights and freedoms of the peasants in the hinterlands, known sometimes as *fueros* (literally, "old customs"). The inevitable struggle between national royal authority and the left-over freedoms of feudal times led to a constant assault upon the *fueros* by successive Hapsburg kings. In 1640 occurred the rebellion of the *segadores* ("hoers") throughout Catalonia, a rebellion supported covertly at first, then openly, by the citizens of Barcelona. But the uprising led only to the ruthless

suppression of the peasants of Catalonia and the conquest of Barcelona itself by royal armies in 1652.

The War of the Segadores was no more than an over-
ture to the wars into which Barcelona was now to be
plunged. Dynastic rivalries and inter-European poli-
tics had brought the Spanish monarchy into conflict
with France—and any war between Spain and France
would have to be fought out in Catalonia, for the Catalan plains were the obvious route for invading armies
to enter Spain. The successive battles and wars of the
seventeenth century were wonderfully complicated,
but as far as Barcelona was concerned they were disastrous. Offering its allegiance to France in 1640, the
city, as we have seen, was recaptured by the Spanish
monarchy in 1652. No immediate punishment was
meted out. Then, in 1697, after years of bloody warfare, the city was again captured by the French but
was restored to Spain by the Treaty of Ryswick. It was
held by various generals on behalf of various claimants
to the Spanish throne during the Wars of the Spanish
Succession but was finally recaptured by Philip V of
Spain in 1714. All during these stormy years the good
citizens of Barcelona had been busily running back and
forth to offer their allegiance to the strongest apparent
force on the horizon, sometimes French, sometimes
Spanish. They reaped the reward of that policy in 1714
when the victorious Philip abolished all the city's ancient rights and privileges, making it all but a colony
of the Spanish crown. The battles fought both within
the city and across the face of Catalonia during this
century of war had impoverished Barcelona. But of
greater impact on the city's former prosperity was the
loss of its Mediterranean trading supremacy to Mar-

seilles in France and Genoa in Italy. Furthermore, Mediterranean trade itself had dwindled to insignificance, having been replaced by transatlantic trade monopolized by English, Dutch and German ports.

It was during the eighteenth century, too, that the guilds of Barcelona were extinguished (except in ceremonial form and function). This was brought about by royal decrees. For example, in 1772 the king authorized any and all foreigners to establish themselves in any craft or trade without any previous examination; in 1778 he decreed that any master craftsman might open an unlimited number of shops; in 1798 the grade of master was thrown open to any citizen without previous examination by any authority whatsoever, thereby eliminating the very grade itself. All of which reflected a struggle between royal and local authority. By undermining the guilds the king was weakening the strongest remaining municipal organizations. It reflected, too, an attack upon the guilds from below—from the increasing number of unskilled, unequipped workers who saw themselves effectively excluded from economic advancement by the rigid guild structure, the remnants of a feudal "closed shop." Basically the death of the guilds, along with the death of the entire medieval, Renaissance and post-Renaissance structure of society was brought about by the emergence of a new economic system—capitalism. As trade and commerce brought new concentrations of capital, as population increased (despite visitations of the plague), as new inventions increased productivity and replaced

*Barcelona has been building ships for two thousand years.*

hand-craftsmanship, and as more and more peasants fled the toilsome land for city life, the capitalist economic system was born. Craftsmen and ex-peasants alike found that they had nothing to sell now but their labor—to those who could afford to build and equip the new factories. The old social structure which, if rigid and hierarchical, at least provided a secure place for every member of the community, was replaced by a social structure based upon exploitation of human and material resources.

Catalonia was well equipped with material resources. The rivers, especially the Ebro, tumbling down from the Pyrenees, would provide power, and there were coal and minerals in the north. Furthermore, Barcelona's unique relationship to France and the world beyond assured that mechanical inventions would reach Catalonia first among all Spanish provinces. That same relationship also assured that the ideas of the French Revolution would be received with greater enthusiasm in Catalonia than anywhere else in Spain, a fact which illuminates the history of the city during the nineteenth century.

For the rest of Spain was late to industrialize and late to understand the new social, economic and political orders implicit in both the French and the Industrial revolutions. The people of Catalonia and Barcelona, already conscious of their separateness in culture from the rest of the nation, now saw Spain as a serious intellectual, spiritual and, above all, economic drag on their future prosperity. When Napoleon's armies invaded the peninsula (first as allies, then as conquerors), many Catalonians welcomed them. But it was soon apparent that the French had come to exploit, not enlighten Spain, and the people of Catalonia and Barcelona joined wholeheartedly in the nation-wide guerrilla war against the French occupation forces which, with the help of English troops under Sir Arthur Wellesley (later Duke of Wellington), finally drove the French back over the Pyrenees in 1814.

But the French presence in Spain was not entirely without benefits. A new spirit of independence and a drive for constitutional democratic political forms had been awakened within the Spanish people. One of the keynotes of Spanish liberalism was to be the attitude it maintained toward the Catalan drive for independence. When the national authority in Madrid was liberal, it would view with favor Catalonia's various self-government schemes; when it was reactionary it would oppose them. Catalonia, and Barcelona, would therefore support any candidate for national authority who appeared to be most liberal. And during the nineteenth century this involved the province and the city on the losing side of the complicated series of civil wars known as the Carlist Wars, which were to rend the fabric of Spanish society all during the century.

There was a deeper significance to the Carlist Wars than simply the drive toward local self-government or political autonomy in Catalonia. For if the rich manufacturers and bankers of Barcelona dreamed of a separation from Spain which would reduce their taxes and expand their trade (increasingly constricted by outmoded national taxation and foreign policies), the greatly expanding industrial working class of the province and the city dreamed of a local, republican, liberal government which would understand and foster their drive toward social justice, economic betterment and mass-participation democracy. Traditionalist Spain, unindustrialized, captive of archaic social and religious attitudes, based primarily on an all-but-feudal agriculture and the victim of unscrupulous politicians and army generals who hid behind the façade of monarchy, was utterly unable to offer progressive solutions to Catalan problems (or to the problems of the rest of Spain). It was no wonder then that, after decades of chaotic conflict between traditionalists and liberals on the national scene, when the two Spains fell upon each other in the bloody Civil War of 1936–1939, Catalonia and Barcelona formed the essential bastion of the Republic. Nor was it surprising that when traditionalist Spain, led by General Francisco Franco, won the Civil War, Catalonia and Barcelona should be severely punished. Like certain of his predecessors, Franco, the inheritor of supreme power in Madrid, not only crippled Catalan industry and Barcelona commerce through taxation, not only inflicted bloody reprisals upon Catalan political and trade-union leaders and wiped out every trace of the Catalan separatist movements, he also attempted to root out that Catalan culture which formed the bedrock of Catalan apartness from the rest of Spain. The Catalan language was forbidden to be taught, Catalan writings from poetry to newspapers were proscribed and a concentrated drive to rewrite and reteach history was undertaken.

All of which failed of its purpose, for Spain needed Barcelona at least as much, probably more, than Barcelona needed Spain. Since the opening of the Suez Canal late in the nineteenth century had once again made Barcelona a key port between Europe and the

The people of Barcelona have had two
millennia to reflect on the fundamentals of
human nature (gambling in this case on
the lottery)—and have decided to put up
with them.

East, and the rapid development of the power and mineral resources of the hinterlands had made Catalonia the industrial center of the peninsula, the prosperity of Spain had come more and more to depend on the prosperity of its errant province and the province's still more errant capital city. With the emergence of tourism as a great national industry, when Barcelona became the funnel through which millions of foreigners poured into the peninsula during the late fifties and sixties, its importance once again outweighed its rebelliousness. Like their forefathers during medieval times, the citizens of Barcelona found themselves able to exact greater and greater rights, privileges and freedoms from a central government which depended upon their trade, commerce and taxes. Until, during very recent years, all the repressive measures imposed by traditionalist Spain in 1939 had vanished, and the people of Barcelona (and Catalonia) were once again masters within their own house.

And that is the shell of history within which a remarkable city was born and reborn many times over; within which generations of people developed an urban style of life still unique in the modern world. That life and the architecture and layout of the city mingle with tradition in complex and colorful patterns. To examine the city in detail is to follow the many still-vital historical threads which have combined in our own day to produce a vivid life-tapestry.

# 2 The Gothic Stage

*Carder's Street, a little bit sore*
*from the showing-off of shop-keepers haughty,*
*scornful tailors or churchgoers naughty,*
*and the Inn of Good Luck's carven door,*
    *is no more!*

                    —GUERAU DE LIOST

There are few cities in the world that preserve their nucleus; almost none in North America. Succeeding generations, through indifference, the greed of exploitation, the real or imagined need for self-assertion, tear down the building of previous eras to replace it with their own just-as-ephemeral construction. Sometimes the destruction is justified, but most often it is not. And in those cities where medieval or even pre-medieval nucleii are to be found, they are most often empty shells, museums inhabited only by caretakers and hordes of tourists. The patterns of life have changed and the original city-stage is no longer suitable for a living drama. Barcelona is a happy exception to this rule. Very much of its medieval core is still stand-

*Plaza de Marqullas—the streets meander, the vistas constantly shift; the eye of the pedestrian can never be bored.*

ing in excellent condition and, most important, is still functioning as an integral part of the way of life of its citizens. People still live in the Gothic Quarter, people still run shops and restaurants there, people still worship there. Despite the busloads of tourists who infest the place, the people of Barcelona do not regard this most ancient center of their city as a museum but as a going concern, as important to the everyday life of Barcelona as any other section of the city.

In fact, it wasn't called the Gothic Quarter until very recently, but simply District Number One of Barcelona. Only the work of recent scholars, archaeologists and medievalists has pinned that name upon the district. But its inhabitants steadfastly refuse to consider themselves Gothic simply because they live in an ancient environment. Furthermore, the Gothic Quarter exerts its influence on the rest of Barcelona not only as a museum or shrine but also as an important functioning part of the whole. Those who live in District Number One and those who visit it either daily or occasionally do not, of course, lead Gothic lives because of its influence. But the existence of an entire Gothic center functioning within Barcelona does have an impact on the way of life of the city and its people —and it does provide them with a stage sadly lacking in most cities, a stage upon which they may be most aware of the ghosts of actors long since vanished.

When Rome's power ebbed out of the old empire a new power was preparing to assert itself amid the ruins and chaos of the previous world order. This was the power of Christianity, and the Gothic city was its fullest expression in actuality. Christians of the fifth and sixth centuries, surrounded by the wreckage of the

Roman world, looked to a heavenly city, a mystical capital whose day would come, and embraced a new mystical-social bond: the communion of saints. Among its other virtues, Christianity could count as primary that of looking at the world in a realistic way. The Christian expected evil—sickness, death, war, pain; even the catastrophic end of the world. And he was right. Instead of avoiding these realities, he sought to sublimate his fear by rushing to accept them. His whole life-drama was a series of negations successfully accepted. He helped the sick and the poor, suffered gladly the loneliness of spiritual contemplation, was eager for the pain of martyrdom. The cities in which he lived were designed as stages and centers for an entirely different outlook from the Roman. He had no use for arenas, for theaters, for forums, for pagan monuments, for public baths. These were the symbols and functions of a detestable (to him) and dying culture. In practically all the cities of the Roman world these public buildings and areas fell into decay with disuse. The only remnants of the pagan city which the Christians found useful and preserved were the ancient temples to the gods, which they converted into churches, basilicas and cathedrals dedicated to their God. Although the barbarian invasions from the third century on brought destruction to the urban civilization of Rome, the social and spiritual content of that urbanism had been steadily eroded from within until, when final catastrophe came in the fifth and sixth centuries, the barbarians were destroying not living cities, but shells.

As people fled from barbarian hordes, plagues, the decay of towns, the mindless violence of no-longer-restrained urban gangsters and mobs, they tried to create on earth a miniature copy of their ideal City of God. In its earliest expression this new concept of civic life gave birth to the monastery, an environment which brought together many like-minded men within a community ordered and structured upon their imagining of the Holy City. It was within the monastery that the ideal purposes of a new urbanism were devised. The monastery was both a link with the knowledge of the past and a proving ground for new social relationships and conceptions, a matrix from which the medieval city would draw inspiration. It was not, however, the nucleus of the new cities themselves. These were, for the most part, destined to rise on the same sites as the old. Social disaster did not alter geography. A natural port city, a naturally defensible civic location, an important crossroads—all these were determining factors in the survival of the pre-Christian urban sites. Nor did a new religion entirely efface the age-old awe and superstition with which most urban centers had long been regarded. Cities which arose first as shrines to the divinity under whose protection their trade and commerce were placed retained their mystical aura; its nature simply changed to conform to Christian belief and usage. And, under the impact of continuing attack from without—from Vikings, Mohammedans, bands of freebooters—the inhabitants of surviving cities once again discovered the virtues of the wall as a defensive unit. The wall never fell asleep on guard duty, and with a little effort and ingenuity it could be made to withstand practically any assault the technology of the age could mount. The crumbled Roman walls of post-Roman Europe were reconstructed and strengthened from the eighth to the twelfth centuries. But not only did the rebuilt walls defend the city— they also gave it definition. And with definition came municipal structure. The combination of surviving awe, protection in a lawless world and renewed civic formalism proved (as it has done throughout history) a powerful magnet, drawing people to the city from ever more distant countrysides. And the medieval city came into being.

The history of Barcelona, as we have seen, reflected the general pattern of decay, destruction, rebirth and emergence into the new medieval order. And its progress may be followed every step of the way in the Gothic Quarter. There are, for example, remnants of the old Roman wall constructed after the third century raid from the north; there are remnants of the later walls built against Moors and rival feudal domains. The old Roman-Christian basilica built (or rather adapted from an earlier temple) in the fourth century, burned by Almanzor during his raid in the tenth century, is still a holy shrine. It is now the Church of Santa Lucia, a pre-Gothic, Romanesque structure. The Feast of Santa Lucia is on December 13th, and on that day a large fair is held outside the church at which all sorts of toys and Christmas decorations (not glistening Christmas tree ornaments, but the little figures of shepherds, kings, animals and the Holy Family with which Barcelona children make their yearly Nativity scenes) are sold. The market-fair is celebrated under the benign protection of Santa Lucia, just as it has been for untold centuries. For the reemergence of the medieval market, free from plundering raids, at which men might have some confidence in the weights and measures, and in each other's good word and trading practices, took place under the protection of the Church; specifically, under the protection of the local bishop. The market-fair of Santa Lucia is a still-vital medieval function of Barcelona's life.

Dominating the Gothic Quarter, as it dominated the life of medieval Barcelona, is the great Cathedral of Santa Eulalia. This is the structure which was started early in the eleventh century and completed in the thirteenth, the church at the dedication of which Ramón Berenguer promulgated Barcelona's Usatges. The vaulted ceilings, lost in high shadows, lead the eye and the mind to contemplation of the infinite; the proliferation of paintings of the lives of the saints, the statues of martyrs and angels remind the beholder of the intervention of God in man's earthly affairs.

The faith upon which this, one of the world's most beautiful cathedrals, was built is still a most important aspect of the life of the city. Catalans, by and large, are born into the Catholic faith, raised and educated in it. Even in the nonreligious public schools much time is set aside for religious studies, and within the national structure of Spain the Catholic Church retains privileges in education and other matters which it long ago lost in every other country in Europe. If the Catalan, due to differences in his history, lacks something of the fanaticism possible in other Spaniards as they approach their religion, if he is sometimes said to be anticlerical, he nevertheless basically remains devoutly Christian. During the Civil War of 1936–1939, when Barcelona crowds looted, burned and devastated churches and monasteries, sometimes killing priests and nuns, their rage was compounded by belief that

*The Cathedral of Santa Eulalia manages to rise superior to the clutter of traffic—a confrontation of faiths.*

the Church in Barcelona was not Christian *enough*, that it had betrayed the teachings of Christ to meddle in mundane affairs and had become a bulwark of the rich and reactionary. The Catalan attitude toward religion may therefore be said to be a mixture of basic Christian faith, anticlericalism and a reformist zeal largely unknown in other lands in which the Church was long ago dethroned from its dominating place in national councils.

But baptisms, communions, marriages, feast days, deaths and many other events are of central importance in the lives of the citizens of Barcelona, and all are intimately bound up with the Church. And since Barcelona churches are both very old and very functional, they are a living and vital link with past generations and ways of behavior. They lend an indispensable sense of continuity to the life of the city, a sense of common belief, of communion in a faith which is still an affair of daily importance. Whether or not an individual believes all that the Church preaches, a feeling of historical, if not philosophical, security is available to him within the ancient stone walls of the cathedrals and basilicas.

The Gothic Quarter of Barcelona rose, and rose again, on the basic plans of the Roman colony. Its street layout was a gridiron originally and, with many modifications, remains so today. But the function of post-Roman streets was not only or even primarily to move traffic, and the function of the medieval city was not efficient exploitation of its terrain. The street was a place where neighbors met in common, where traffic was mostly afoot, where personal, individual contact between people took place. If medieval streets were narrow, they were wide enough for their purpose. Many of the streets in the Gothic Quarter today are closed to all except pedestrians. And in walking rather than riding through them, people have the opportunity of seeing in detail (and being affected by) the work of architects, sculptors and artisans. Proposals to demolish graceful old buildings in favor of more mechanically functional structures therefore run into a stone wall of public disapproval based upon very personal as well as theoretical attachments to the presence of the past.

The modifications of the gridiron Roman layout of the Gothic Quarter by the introduction of cathedrals, palaces, monasteries, and by the usages of time and the destructions of various wars were basically the imposition of more humane concepts of life upon an older concept of naked power. Streets in the Gothic Quarter curve, wind, tangle upon themselves. They are not thoroughfares for armies to march upon—armies dedicated to the power of the state, or armies of automobiles dedicated to the power of the machine. They are foot routes for people. Like people they sometimes contradict themselves; like people they have a way of getting confused, losing the thread of their arguments; like people they are intimate, and like people they are full of surprises. Looking down a Gothic Quarter street the pedestrian is not reminded of his impotence in a geometrical, mechanistic universe, but rather of his common humanity and his importance as an individual. Most vistas end not in open, distant horizons, but in the sudden interposition of a building or the beckoning sunlight and shade of small garden plazas. Such streets are not places to be shunned, as the broad traffic-filled avenues of modern cities are shunned, but places to be enjoyed. They do not suggest power, speed, noise, inhuman efficiency; they suggest leisure, conversation, contemplation and individual, personal contact. As such they are more successfully functional than the streets of New York, London, Moscow or even of the Victorian section of Barcelona itself. And since the citizens of Barcelona are still governed from the town hall of the Gothic Quarter, still attend its churches and wander through its museums, still seek bargains in its thousands of small shops, still live in many of its ancient buildings, they are brought into constant daily touch with a conception of life and of the human being far different from that expressed by younger sections of the city.

The Gothic Quarter of Barcelona contains no park— medieval cities did not have parks. Since the entire city was designed as a place in which people could meet at leisure and since the countryside was within easy walking distance just beyond the encircling wall, there was no need for parks. But the provision of natural greenery was not overlooked. Gothic Quarter houses, palaces and the great Cathedral itself are built around inner courtyards in which flowers, trees and shrubs are carefully cultivated. The idea is simply a repetition of the layout of post-Roman monasteries, castles and the city itself; central food-producing land surrounded by defensive masonry. With the cultivation of food in larger areas outside the walls, the idea of a garden for beauty and pleasure replaced the concept of a garden for subsistence; and with the substitution of a city-girdling rather than a private wall, the surrounding masonry was not for defense but for habitation. In the

*Calle de la Paz* in the
Gothic Quarter—a street on
the human scale.

case of palaces or the houses of the very rich, these gardens were and remain private. But most were the common gardens of many poor families living in the buildings around them.

Open green space was also provided organically by the small squares and plazas formed by the junctions of several streets, or reserved for the necessary gathering of people at public functions. Very often the squares in front of churches were descendants of common-market places. Here peasants from the countryside and artisans from all over the city could set up their open-air stalls on certain days to sell and barter their wares. As we have seen, at certain times and places they still do. These same squares provided room for people to assemble at important religious observances or on civic occasions. The Plaza San Jaime, for example, planned and situated between the provincial palace and the town hall, was the place at which a general assembly of citizens could gather to hear of new laws or to approve or disapprove of actions taken by the municipal government.

Many of the small plazas and squares of medieval Barcelona were built around fountains. The fountain was the medieval water-supply system. Hollowed-out logs led water from the Llobregat and the Besós into the city proper and to several central distribution points. From there householders carried it home in buckets. If this system had its inconveniences, it also had two very definite civic advantages. First, the fountain provided the occasion for a work of art—most were designed around sculpted sea themes, such as Triton and his porpoises. Secondly, the fountain was a social gathering place where housewives came to gossip while awaiting their turn to fill jars and buckets for the home.

Markets, too, served as more than food-distribution centers. Held in various of the city squares, their wares were displayed from open stalls tended by the people who had actually grown the food, woven the cloth, imported the silks and spices. Bargaining between buyer and seller, the exchange of personal contact on all levels, made marketing a social occasion and reinforced the sense of civic unity.

In what ways has the continued existence of this Gothic stage influenced the development and life of modern Barcelona? It is difficult to distinguish the survival of architectural style and medieval reminders from the many economic, political and accidental factors that have influenced the city's growth over the centuries. But certain influences seem clear.

First of all, the conception of the city as a work of art, as a consciously contrived stage upon which the urban civic drama takes place, is one which must occur to most citizens living within or nearby such a splendid example as the Gothic Quarter. In very many, perhaps most, modern cities, architects, sculptors, muralists, gardeners have an all but impossible task to convince a significant group of their fellow citizens that beauty for its own sake is an essential ingredient in town planning. But not in Barcelona. The many, many buildings decorated with statues and murals and colored tiles which were erected in the centuries following the

*The uses of a fountain in public space—refreshment, décor, social intercourse.*

explosion of the city beyond its medieval walls bear testimony to this. It seems quite natural to a citizen of Barcelona to pay taxes for the erection of a statue or the adornment of a new church with intricate filigree ironwork. It seems natural to him that new buildings should make provision for gardens and that these gardens should be designed for beauty—that they should be composed of flowers and shrubs rather than simply vast lawns planted only to comply with the demands of a civic building code. Questions arising from the proposed demolition of old structures or the erection of new engage widespread attention in Barcelona and are the subjects of heated debate in newspapers and at cafés. Private property speculators, corporations intent upon erecting new headquarters, all who would change the urban scene however modestly must take an informed and interested public opinion into account.

Directly and intimately affecting the way of life of every inhabitant of the city is the attitude, derived from medieval times and reinforced by the continuing existence of a Gothic stage, toward the uses of public streets. We have seen that the medieval street was a meeting place as well as a route, a very long public amphitheater. And a very high proportion of Barcelona's streets beyond the Gothic Quarter remain just that. The center of the road has been usurped by traffic, but the sidewalks accommodate outdoor cafés by the hundreds—where people pass the time of day not only to meet friends, transact business, relax, eat or drink, but also, and for our purposes most significantly, in the full confidence and awareness that the street is a fine place to enjoy oneself. There is the ever-fascinating parade of passers-by, the ever-changing kaleidoscope of urban life at close hand. The streets of post-medieval Barcelona are, in other words, not merely arteries for traffic but also places to which it seems most natural for citizens to go for purely personal enjoyment. And this in turn deeply affects urban architecture. The idea that street space is to be consumed by buildings which make no provision for outdoor cafés on their ground floor, or for gardens or small shops, is one that raises instinctive repugnance in people who for centuries have considered the street their personal-public meeting place. Architects must also be aware that their buildings will not be simply glimpsed by passing motorists at high speed or by hurrying pedestrians whose one idea is to get off the street, or by civic commissions that will study them as idealized models on architects' display tables—they will be long and deeply studied by thousands of people sitting just across the street from them in an outdoor café or a garden or a plaza.

The classic example of a street for human use as well as traffic is undoubtedly the series of short connecting avenues in Barcelona known as the Ramblas. Leading from the sea to Plaza Cataluña and then farther into the Victorian sections of the city, the Ramblas are basically very broad boulevards, the centers of which are devoted to pedestrian malls. Or they are pedestrian malls flanked by narrow passages for motor traffic. On the Ramblas there is no question as to who gets priority. It is often faster to walk down the center of these avenues than to drive down their sides. The central malls are not fenced and reserved from people (as are the much narrower dividing sections of New York's

Park Avenue, for example). They are not reserved for shops, as are the new pedestrian malls of some American suburbs and of post World War II Amsterdam. They are reserved for the pleasure of pedestrians who are presumed to enjoy their immediate environment, not merely to hurry through it. There are small market stalls along certain sections at which flowers, pets, books and magazines are sold—fractional elements of a sort of commercialized zoo and garden and library guaranteed to provide interest to those who stroll past them. There are benches upon which the foot-weary may rest; there are outdoor café tables (served from the cafés across the street behind them by daring, traffic-defying, nimble-footed waiters) from which pedestrians can watch the passing parade over a drink or where they can meet friends "accidentally," without the formality of timed appointments (or where, if an appointment has been made, they can sit in comfort to await friends rather than stand harassed on some busy street corner). Nor is this tremendous concession to pedestrians made on some unimportant back street. The Ramblas are the very heart and main artery of Barcelona. They can be compared only to New York's Broadway, Chicago's Lake Shore Drive, Los Angeles' Wilshire Boulevard. And the Ramblas are a natural development from medieval life. The small open-air stalls descend from the stalls of the medieval marketplace, the outdoor cafés are simply sophisticated versions of the sidewalk food and drink vendors of medi-

*The influence of the sidewalk café on the quality of life cannot be overestimated.*

eval times. The entire conception of the street as public theater derives from medieval conceptions of urbanity.

The citizens of Barcelona sometimes refer to the Gothic Quarter as the Casco Antiguo, the "ancient shell," of their city. It is that, of course, in a strict sense. Until the eighteenth century Barcelona continued to be defined by its medieval walls. But in a broader sense the ancient shell was also the container of a seed—the seed of a mode of urban living. Present-day Barcelona is very largely the fruit of that seed.

# 3 The Urban Battlefield

*Citizens of all ages were gifted in both the*
*liberal and applied arts by which the city*
*flourished. People without jobs did not exist,*
*they all had their occupations. For this reason*
*there were no poor people, and all the people*
*lived correctly and with plenty of money.*

—LUCIO MARINEO SICULO

At least, so it appeared to a visitor in the year 1484, in
the decade that saw the signs and symbols of the end
of feudal order and felt the rumblings of something
new and, as yet, undefined on the social horizon. But
it would be well to remember that even during Barcelona's Gothic glory, not everybody lived correctly and
with plenty of money. There was always an unraveling
edge of poverty and misery to the gorgeous tapestry of
medieval life. For example, all those (and they were
many) who, for lack of skill or will or luck did not be-
long to the guilds which monopolized production; all
those struck down by disease in an age when plagues
were common; all those crippled or maimed at a time
when human strength was the source of industrial

power; all those who fell afoul of harsh feudal law or the intricacies of Christian dogma—all were outcasts and victims. Not all the buildings in Gothic Barcelona were palaces, churches or guildhalls. Many were wooden, straw-roofed, dirt-floored shanties into which crowded the miserable families of the poor. And if the streets were delightful meeting places, they were also, toward the close of the Middle Ages (when scavenging animals such as pigs and chickens were no longer permitted to roam freely), open, stinking sewers. The plazas and squares were not only statuary-studded gardens—too often they were the settings for autos-da-fé, during which agents of the Church burned witches, heretics and masses of the "unfaithful." The palaces of the counts of Barcelona and the kings of Aragón contained not only elegant reception halls but also tiny rat-infested, earth-embedded dungeons in which to inter political enemies.

But evidence of medieval cruelty, disease and poverty no longer mars the Gothic Quarter. Wooden huts do not survive time and fire; dungeons become historical curiosities, and it is hard to imagine the well-tiled pavement beneath your feet as formerly a mud-and-filth-soaked sewer. What has survived is the beautiful shell of medieval life to remind succeeding generations of what men once conceived a city to be. No matter that the medieval conception of the city as "Christianopolis," the heavenly city on earth, had not been fully realized: it was at least a noble idea. But it was an idea, a conception of urban life, that died with the coming of the commercial-industrial age. It was to be replaced by the concept of the city as a site for exploitation, and this concept also was to be recorded in brick and stone and concrete as an expression of the new urban order. The Gothic stage remained, but beyond it grew up a new stage on which people consciously and unconsciously enacted new roles. This stage did not retain the organic unity of Gothic design; it reflected the disunity of increasingly polarized social relationships. This disunity, the fragmentation of society under the impact of the rise of capitalism and industrialization, transformed the civic theater into an arena of competition and, eventually, a battlefield.

The fragmentation started earlier than might be supposed. Gothic Barcelona was defined by its great wall, one length of which ran down to the sea along those broad avenues today known as the Ramblas. But as early as the fourteenth century a new quarter was rising beyond this section of the wall. It was the home of the artisans who worked in the great shipyards known as the Atarazanas, and also the area in which the huddled shanties of sailors and dockworkers sprang up. Because land was cheap beyond the walls, and because the waterfront was as close as the shipyards, the new commercial trading companies that grew during the fourteenth to sixteenth centuries built their headquarters there, too. Since much of their trade was with the Orient, the entire section eventually came to be called the Barrio Chino. It was (and remains) one of the world's earliest examples of the commercial-industrial slum.

The streets of the Barrio Chino, like those of the Gothic Quarter, are narrow, winding and full of surprises. But among those surprises are not to be found garden-squares or plazas (except in front of the very old church of San Pablo del Campo—its name, St. Paul

*The older merchants' houses of the Barrio
Chino have long since been abandoned
to commercial functions.*

of the Fields, recalling a time when the church rose in the countryside beyond the walls). For land here was always looked upon as exploitable—exploitable for rents from the workers jammed into crowded hovels and as commercial sites for businesses. At a very early date the men who owned the businesses—merchants, shipbuilders, marine insurance brokers—no longer lived (as did the master craftsmen of the Gothic Quarter) over their stores or above their headquarters. They lived elsewhere, either within the walls or, later, within the rings of suburbs which grew up beyond the walls to the west. No one of money or influence had any intrinsic interest in beautifying the Barrio Chino. Its filthy alleys and crumbling slum-dwellings reflected a social structure in which men no longer saw transcendental order or purpose. No one was responsible for anyone else; civic organization such as that represented by the vanishing guilds was replaced by commercial competition; a social order based on cooperation and hierarchy was replaced by one based on individual greed.

Not all at once, of course. The death of the feudal civic order was accomplished over many centuries. For example, within the Barrio Chino were erected, up until the sixteenth century, Church-administered hospitals and orphanages, the monks of various orders continuing their charitable functions in increasing isolation. The Hospital of Santa Cruz, finished in 1415 (reconstructed in 1638 after a fire), re-created the walled-cloister motif which had been the original seed of the Gothic city. But while, in earlier centuries, the cloister had been the model from which the surrounding urban center drew its inspiration, by the fifteenth century it was once again isolated within the community. The central gardens, the porticos, the covered walks of Santa Cruz express in architecture the old concept of Christian order. But the surrounding streets and mass of urban buildings do not harmonize with it. They ignore it, and in their formless, planless jumble form a sea of architectural disorder (reflecting social and civic disorder) around an island of tranquility.

The breakdown of medieval civic order which gave rise to the slums of the Barrio Chino was formalized, after the severe struggles of the sixteenth and seventeenth centuries, by the replacement of urban power by royal, national power. During those centuries the many sieges and conquests of Barcelona by Castilian and French armies reflected not only the national contests between Spain and France but, as we have seen, a desperate attempt by the people of Barcelona and Catalonia to reassert their former independence of either. In this they failed, and their failure also found architectural and civic expression. If the rich of Barcelona had turned to exploiting their fellow citizens, the kings of Spain found means of exploiting the entire city. The prime symbols of this subordination of civic to national authority remain in the castle of Montjuich, the surviving buildings of Ciudadela and the organized slum of Barceloneta.

Since the days of the Carthaginians there had always been some sort of fortification on Montjuich. The hill offered the best site for command of the harbor and a natural outpost for defense of the city from the south. But during the seventeenth and eighteenth centuries the complex of older forts and remains of walls were incorporated into a formal fortress under royal, na-

*The fortress of Montjuich—symbol of national domination of the city; now a military museum.*

tional control. And since the new guns of Montjuich had only Spain itself to fire upon toward the south, there was little doubt that they were installed to control the city to the north and west. Like the Norman's Tower, built to dominate independent London, Montjuich was fortified to dominate rebellious Barcelona. When the city rose against royal authority, it was the fortress of Montjuich which was the first objective, and, unlike the Tower of London, Montjuich fell from time to time to citizen armies.

The idea of an independently powerful city-state, which died hard in Barcelona (if it can be said to be finally dead at all), has also adorned the city in unexpected ways. For its support of the "wrong" pretender to the Spanish crown during the interminable and complex wars of the seventeenth century, Barcelona was punished by the finally triumphant Philip V in 1714. In that year, after the end of one of the many dreadful sieges which the city had sustained, the conquering Philip, deciding that Montjuich was not sufficient protection against his rebellious subjects, simply detached a large part of the city and made it into a royal stronghold. Known as Ciudadela ("little city"), the whole area north and east of the Gothic Quarter was sequestered, walled and turned over to the military authorities. More than 1,250 houses as well as many churches and convents were thereby amputated from Barcelona. A royal governor's palace was constructed, hundreds of cannons were emplaced along the new walls, houses were converted into barracks and a military city-within-a-city came into being. Caught between Ciuadela and Montjuich, the citizens of Barcelona were forcefully given to understand that civic independence had been ground out between the upper and nether royal millstones.

In the long run, however, the royal seizure and fortification of Ciudadela proved to be a stroke of luck for the city. By the middle of the nineteenth century, when it appeared that the military domination of Barcelona by means of the cannon of Ciudadela was no longer needful or practical, this vast area, having been for nearly two centuries under national rather than civic control, was available for development free from private commercial interests. Accordingly, under the direction of José Fontsere, with royal support and civic approval, Ciudadela was transformed into a park. The former arsenal, the governor's palace and certain other buildings were retained as museums. The Plaza de Armas, where the royal regiments had paraded, was made into a garden, and the whole area was landscaped, dotted with fountains, lakes, paths and a remarkably large and complete zoo.

If the imposition of royal authority was accidentally to give Barcelona one of the world's most beautiful parks in later years, the solidification of national, centralized power was also to scar the city. Of course one man's scar may be another's improvement. Perhaps the most revealing and important symbol of the new age of power and capital which began with the peace of 1714 was the avenue. Broad, wide, straight boulevards leading to infinitely remote horizons; highways for the tremendous increase in wheeled vehicles of the eighteenth century but, more importantly, reviewing grounds for national armies. Royal regiments, if their appearance is to be effective (and it must be effective in order to overawe the populace), need broad, straight grounds on which to march in precision. Furthermore, the older medieval streets, narrow and winding and likely as not paved with handy cobblestones, were a grave danger to an organized army. Citizens could raise havoc with troops through the use of barricades, etc. To be effective an army needs space to maneuver, such space as wide avenues provide. Avenues cut through and around a city provide means of easy military access and control. The broad, straight Paseo Maritimo which (under various names) girdles Barcelona along the sea, was laid out, paved and widened (it is very wide) during the early eighteenth century. Fittingly enough, it led straight to the military encampment of Ciudadela. It was during this time, too, that the series of broad Ramblas were rationalized and clearly defined, cutting between the old Gothic Quarter and the Barrio Chino. Streets leading into the Gothic Quarter itself (principally Calle de Fernando) and the broad boulevard Via Layetana bordering the Quarter on the north were straightened, paved and cut ruthlessly through existing structures.

In this new concept of the uses of a street, buildings formed a setting for the avenue itself. On each side of the boulevard the buildings stood stiff and erect like soldiers, and in themselves were meant to overbear the stroller or spectator. Such, for example, was the new palace of the civil governor built in 1790 along the waterfront boulevard, appropriately designed by a military engineer (the Count of Roncali), meant to house the apparatus of royal control which had usurped

*The subtropical informality of Ciudadela Park*

the powers of the old civic administration. It is a taste-less but "grand" building, a fitting companion to the various port administration and customs buildings which stretch stolidly down the waterfront avenues, blocking off much of the sea view, giving a ponderous, bureaucratic appearance to the whole. Just beyond the civil governor's palace stands the main railroad sta-tion, the Station of France, with broad tracks leading north, an edifice constructed during the late nineteenth century with the lack of taste normally displayed in Victorian industrial architecture.

Beyond the broad, military boulevards of the water-front, forming one of the arms enclosing Barcelona harbor, lies the area known as Barceloneta ("little Barcelona"), consciously constructed as barracks-slum housing for industrial workers in the middle of the eighteenth century. Previous to this time the area had been one vast beach to which the populace could re-pair during hot summer months. Now, once again un-der the authority of military engineers and royal archi-tects (specifically, the Captain-General of Catalonia, the Marqués de la Mina), the entire district was laid out like a military encampment—nine streets drawn parallel to the sea and fifteen built exactly perpendicu-lar to them. The houses, true barracks, were limited to one floor and their fronts were all exactly the same. Later, when the workers who were jammed into these barracks overflowed the living space, an additional floor was decreed for every building in the area. In essence, this was a very early housing project, and but for the fact that it was only two stories high, was built with the same fine disregard of every human and aes-thetic value which has marked most public housing projects throughout the world ever since. But it was certainly efficient. By the eighteenth century the shipyards had spread from the waterfront of the Barrio Chino all the way north to Barceloneta; the new national customs houses were there, and so, too, were the warehouses. The first industrial factories were beginning to encroach north of the district, and the main road (later the railroad) to France carried produce north. In other words, Barceloneta provided housing for the masses of workers needed exactly in the area in which it was built. Of course it quickly became a dreadful slum, but unlike the slums of the Barrio Chino, it was directly and easily accessible to army and police, and thus easily controllable.

References to royal and national authority as the agencies of transforming Barcelona beyond the Gothic Quarter should not mislead us into supposing that government officials and military men and bureaus were acting either in a vacuum or for themselves directly. They were the instruments of control of a new society —one which openly exploited human as well as material resources and was based on the private ownership of every means of production and of every necessity of life. This was the early or "paleotechnic" capitalist society which grew up with the Industrial Revolution—a revolution that came late to Spain and to Catalonia. It was mostly for the benefit of the rich, for the financiers and factory owners and their managers and directors, that the broad avenues were built, the organized barracks-slums for workers provided, the new "palaces" of finance (like the Customs House) and civic administration created. The royal, national or provincial authority which imposed these changes on Barcelona

*Victorian steel spider-web-work roofs
the Station of France.*

was only acting for the benefit of its principal supporters.

If military control, commercial aggrandizement and industrial exploitation created the inhumanly broad avenues and the slums of Barceloneta, they also created an entirely new city west of the old one—a new city for the rich. Fine country houses and estates had grown up since the seventeenth century in the districts west of the Gothic Quarter and the Barrio Chino. And in the middle of the nineteenth century this entire area was rationalized and redesigned (again by a military engineer, Ildefonso Cerda). It is known as the Ensanche (literally, "belt"), as it once formed an outer residential belt to the west of the older districts. Here the new town houses of the rich were constructed. And, of course, the streets were laid out with an overwhelmingly monotonous fidelity to plain geometry. They are all straight, perpendicular to each other and form exactly equidimensional residential blocks. There are no parks or gardens in the Ensanche—the houses of the rich had their own private gardens. The streets are all exactly twenty meters wide, the houses (although, since they were privately constructed, they display differing façades) are so similar as to confuse people looking for a particular address. But the entire district is removed from the sight, smell and sound of the factories from which its wealth was drawn. Businessmen living in the Ensanche had no need to be aware of the hideous slums growing up in other parts of the city; they lived a suburban life, abandoning the central city to commerce, industry, and the makeshift life of the poor. The point at which the Ensanche touched older Barcelona, after a severe struggle between the advocates of geometry and the partisans of more humane city planning, was built as an unhappy compromise between the two. This is the vast and monumental Plaza Cataluña, a plaza so large as to be almost a small park (its vistas, then, no longer intimate and warm), planted squarely between the terminus of the old Ramblas and the beginnings of the new broad Ensanche avenues. There are charming fountains, little plots of formal gardens, benches and pigeons; this much is conceded to the old conception of a plaza. But the entire plaza is surrounded by the large, ponderous buildings that house Catalan and Spanish bank headquarters and is circled by very wide and busy boulevards. The plaza itself, its surrounding buildings and avenues are all far beyond the human scale. Furthermore, people strolling through it or simply sitting in the sun or feeding the pigeons cannot help but be aware that they are surrounded by the symbols of finance and power—housed in suitably huge and ugly buildings. The plaza is not a place of rest and contemplation; it is a place of hurried meetings, traffic and the odor of business.

The Barrio Chino, Barceloneta, Ciudadela, the boulevards, the factories, and the Ensanche are some of the physical manifestations of the inner change in society that succeeded the medieval order. What can they tell us of the changes in the daily life and outlook of the people of the city?

First of all, take the function of the street itself. In medieval times, it was primarily a meeting place also accommodated to foot traffic. Here the rich and the poor jostled together—on the street, in the plazas, at the street-stall markets. A rich man might ride on horseback or in a sedan chair, but he could not avoid

*The Plaza Cataluña—unhappy compromise
between human and commercial needs*

contact with the poor all about him. Nor did he necessarily seek to do so. A man's wealth or lack of it might place him in the social hierarchy, but everyone was part of a social order. With the development of the wide avenue the disassociation of the rich from the poor achieves concrete form. The rich man rides in a horse-drawn carriage down the middle of the street while the poor man walks along its edges, in the gutter first, after 1850 on a special strip created for him, the sidewalk. Rich and poor gape at each other—different species in a polarized society. And the carriages of the rich are improved to achieve ever greater speed. Transportation becomes ever more rapid, the idea of movement in the street becomes the idea of "getting somewhere fast."

Take the decay of the Barrio Chino. Although it was never exactly an attractive place to live, yet during the early centuries after the Renaissance, it did boast of some great houses. These were the homes of the merchants who did business in and from that quarter, often from their homes. But as the area became more and more a site for direct exploitation, the rich moved out, leaving their fine houses to decay into warehouses, small factories or slum housing. The rich man could afford to travel to his work; the poor man could not. The poor had to remain in the area near their jobs. And, with the withdrawal of the rich and influential, the entire district was allowed to fall into abysmal poverty and crime. Further polarization of society.

Perhaps the most dramatic example of the new order in Barcelona is the construction of Barceloneta. Here the rich and the government constructed what was little better than an industrial concentration camp to exploit the poor—now creatures apparently of a different species.

The concept of a transcendental order to society, based on Christian values and hierarchy, had, by the beginning of the eighteenth century, all but completely disappeared. Lip service to Christianity was still paid (and the rich often assuaged their consciences by donating hospitals, schools or museums to the community for the use of the poor), but true worship was given now to power. The power of the national authority expressed in its armies, military camps and palaces; the power of money expressed in the steaming factories, palatial residences of the rich and the division of the city into wealthy suburbs and central slums. In architecture the wealthy expressed ever greater extremities of individualism. For example, the department store magnate Eusebio Guëll, at the close of the nineteenth century, hired the great Catalan architect Antoni Gaudí to design his private dwelling— just off the Ramblas in the Barrio Chino (briefly fashionable again in the perverse way decayed areas of a city become fascinating to the rich surfeited by riches) —and was mightily pleased by the twisting stone façade, the gargoyles and colored tile designs, the surrealistic fantasy in stone which resulted. So pleased, in fact, that he later commissioned Gaudí to landscape and decorate a large park (which Guëll donated to the city) north of the Ensanche. It is a place full of architectural jokes (grottoes whose pillars are all slightly askew, concrete garden furniture made of broken bottles and fragments of discarded tiles, boulders peering from the ground with faces carved into them, and so on), a delightful and wholly unique adventure in ima-

*Gaudí's Cathedral of The Holy Family, still
uncompleted, is a curious expression of
frozen faith and inverted middle-class taste.*

gination, one of the great parks of the world. But like all of Gaudí's work, it is more than somewhat excessive; there is a hint of something desperate struggling for life through the tortured stone. And despite the fact that the park was later given to the ciy, all this work was strictly for private consumption. Nor were the wealthy satisfied to observe the forms of an older worship at the ancient cathedral in the Gothic Quarter. Instead they commissioned Gaudí to construct a new cathedral right in the middle of the Ensanche, the Cathedral of the Holy Family, and it, too, partakes of ostentation and twisted inversion of feeling, looking like nothing so much as a volcanic explosion of lava frozen into towers.

Note the fragmentation of social purpose, now almost complete. Art is no longer public. Just as architecture is private, so, too, painting which once splashed form and color on public walls in frescoes or adorned public places such as cathedrals, the town hall, the guildhalls, is now done on canvas and hung behind walls for the private enjoyment of those who can afford it. The theater, once a popular festival in which all classes delighted, is now the preserve of those who can afford tickets. Open-air plays are no longer given in the plazas in front of churches; instead, formal drama and opera is now housed in the expensive confines of the Teatro Lyrico or the Teatro Lyceo and the only part of the drama open to the public at large is the arrival and departure of the gorgeously dressed patrons.

Not that the pleasures of the poor are completely overlooked. Just as ancient Rome provided circuses for the populace, so, too, Barcelona provided bullrings, an amusement park (on the slopes beneath the fortress

of Montjuich), and museums into which the con-
science-stricken rich might pour some of their belong-
ings after they died.

Nor must it be thought that this new manifestation
of power-worship is the exclusive prerogative of the
rich. On the contrary, it is every man's ambition precisely to be rich. Since the goal of life is neither to be
one with God nor to be one with one's fellow men,
then the goal must be individual, material gain, and
the poor man determined enough will pursue that goal
within the new social logic. The city, in short, has become a battlefield of all men against all men. A new
urban stage has been created on which men are to
enact a new urban drama—not the old Gothic morality
play, but the new capitalist-industrial immorality play.

The drama was a long time in rehearsal. Riots, erupt-
ing with increasing frequency from the central city
(the Barrio Chino, the industrial slums north of Ciudadela, Barceloneta) into the Ensanche and the neutral zones of the Ramblas, took place all through the
closing decades of the nineteenth century. But the real
curtain-raiser came on September 24, 1893, when an
anarchist tossed a bomb at a parade of troops. (The
wide, straight avenues, the bands, the numbed by-
standers, the precision of the regiments had evidently
lost their power to impress.) The assassin was caught
and executed, of course. But he was avenged a few
weeks later, on November 8th, when another anarchist
tossed two bombs into the Teatro Lyçeo, killing twen-
ty-two and wounding scores of opera patrons. The
government responded by arresting hundreds, tossing
them into the dungeons of Montjuich and systematic-
ally torturing them to death. Even this repression was

*Barcelona's principal bullring, where older rites of sacrifice are celebrated on Sunday afternoons.*

not enough. Three years later, on June 7, 1896, an anarchist tossed a bomb at the religious procession of Corpus Christi (in the past that would have been a procession in which all the people of the city marched; now it was a procession of the rich and their attendants), killing eleven and frightening the bishop and the commanding general of Barcelona. Wholesale arrests and executions duly followed. Then, in 1909, the underground Labor Federation of Barcelona called a strike to protest the drafting of soldiers from Barcelona to fight a colonialist war in Morocco. The strike turned unexpectedly into a disorganized mass outpouring of the population, which seized control of the central city, and was put down amid scenes of indescribable brutality and bloodshed during what came to be known as La Semana Tragica (the tragic week) of Barcelona. A few decades later, in 1936, when the two Spains—traditionalist and liberal—fell upon each other in the fury of nationwide civil war, it was not to be wondered that Barcelona was the center and vital heart of Republican Spain. Its fall in 1939 to the armies of the traditionalists, led by General Francisco Franco, marked the real death of the Republic, and the loss of another round in an old battle. It also closed another chapter in the continuing urban drama, leaving the stage clear for the next act, one which is still in progress.

It is not, however, our purpose to trace the intricacies of political warfare, which also had extra-urban causes and embraced, after all, not only Barcelona but all Spain. It is important to note in the present context that the ideals and attitudes which expressed themselves in the layout of the city as a center for exploitation produced, eventually, a drama of outright warfare. This is a drama which seems to be opening in American cities today.

People living under the most appalling conditions of poverty, all but imprisoned in industrial ghettos, seeing in other sections of the city the ostentatious display of the wealthy, their means of protest limited either politically or economically, turn to violence as their final response to intolerable conditions. This violence is not restrained by any feeling of fellowship for other citizens of the city; those feelings have long since been extinguished. It may be regarded as a war waged between the central city and its suburbs (in the case of Barcelona, Barceloneta, the Barrio Chino and the industrial slums versus the Ensanche). The strongholds of the poor are capable of withstanding a siege. And when they rebel, the army and the police must conduct regular siege operations against them, followed by house-to-house fighting. This is the final, terrible price to be paid for urban-social fragmentation. It was a price paid in full by the unhappy people of Barcelona over many bloody decades.

The urban drama of force and violence in Barcelona was ended by force and violence in 1939—and that might have meant the stagnation and decline of the city, as it has meant the dwindling of other cities in other places and other times. It has not. For Barcelona was (and remains) fortunate in that other, older traditions have survived the eighteenth to twentieth century inferno. These traditions, customs and civic attitudes have, through the brilliance and energy of its people, been reinterpreted and recast to form the materials for a new urban drama, one based on integration rather than fragmentation and one which finds architectural and planning expression throughout the old and new quarters of the city. But before attending this new drama it would be well to see first how the theater itself functions today.

# 4 Barcelona Backstage

*Article 6: All residents will participate equally or proportionately in municipal services, in communal advantages and in those rights and benefits conceded of a general character.*

—MUNICIPAL ORDINANCES, 1966

And there are few cities in the world where the people participate more actively, consciously and argumentatively in the civic metabolism. By civic, or urban, metabolism we mean the way the city feeds, clothes, lights, heats, houses and cleans itself. And much else. Urban metabolism is everything from the amount of hay delivered to the elephants in the zoo to the number of square yards of paved streets washed daily; from the quantity and quality of its exports to the number of books in circulation among its libraries. All of which can be studied as cold statistics, sociological generalizations, civic abstractions. But implicit in the figures and reports, the graphs and charts of urban metabolism, lie clues to a city's way of life, its attitude toward itself, the personal, individual joys and tragedies of its inhabitants.

What, for example, causes some people in a city, any city, to commit suicide? The municipal statisticians of Chicago or Los Angeles or London, inhabiting the abstract world of their sociological tables, supply answers (when they can) such as "extreme poverty" or "psychiatric unbalance." Such answers assume that the unfortunates involved are victims of life or social forces beyond their control—isolated individuals among a mass, reacting to mass pressures. But among the reasons given for the eighty-six suicides which took place in Barcelona in 1968, in the official municipal statistical guide to that city, are, "disgust with life," "reverses of fortune," "bad luck," and—"unrequited love." In other words, some people at least are granted the final dignity of having consciously chosen to become statistics for deeply personal reasons. And if such statistical distinctions sound more like the libretto for a grand opera than the sober calculations of an impersonal city department, it is because the sense of the dignity of the individual, of his conscious participation in an urban drama, still flourishes in Barcelona.

The personal touch, the individual eccentricity, are still mightily important in the metabolism of this city. Take, for example, the means whereby Barcelona feeds itself. Some 55,000 tons of meat per year are consumed (of which 11,000 tons are frozen meats from Argentina); 77,000 tons of fish; 180,000 tons of vegetables; 171,000 tons of fruits. Most of this produce is brought into the city by ship or rail or truck by large transport companies. The meats are slaughtered and quartered at the municipal slaughterhouse, the vegetables and

*Marketing as social intercourse at the huge Central Market off the Ramblas*

fruits go to the central fruit and vegetable market, a vast, sprawling warehouse between the Gothic Quarter and Ciudadela. But from these central supply sources, most food goes to open-air (or glass-roofed) central markets where it is bought fresh from individual stall owners by individual customers. An example is the very large central market right on the Ramblas—a huge glass-and-steel-covered collection of stalls displaying everything from shrimp to flowers, from meat to snails and all imaginable vegetables and fruits. Any given stall specializes in one thing or another. The food is inspected, weighed (and the price is complained of) and sold, person to person, and carted away by housewives in shopping carts or baskets. Nothing is packaged here, nothing artificially colored. No advertising displays catch the eye; only the beautifully variegated color of the foods, their heavy odors, the importunate cries of the fishwives (traditionally, only fishwives call out to passers-by, never vegetable or meat vendors) distract the customer's attention. Of course people come here to buy food. But they also come here to enjoy the sights, sounds and smells incidental to a stroll through the market, to chat with their favorite vendors, to meet friends (and perhaps have a drink and a snack at one of the several open-air bars and snack counters dotted through the market). In short, shopping in such an atmosphere is a social occasion—an occasion of interpersonal contact.

The great, open central markets (there are more than a dozen in Barcelona), are direct descendants of the street markets and street fairs of the Middle Ages. And if the sense of civic unity and civic dedication that illumined medieval life has so largely vanished, some idea of its pleasures can still be found in its surviving marketing institutions. It is undoubtedly for this reason that Barcelona has so stoutly resisted the invasion of supermarkets. There are many thousands of private stores, of course, aside from the central markets; butchers, bakers, delicatessens, fish shops and vegetable stores. But these are, for the most part, owned by individual families. Furthermore, their wares are displayed and sold in much the same manner as they would be in the central markets. Canned goods in prodigious variety and quantity are available on their shelves, but far fewer are sold than in any American city. It is not only the suspicion with which Barcelona housewives regard packaged foods that causes this, it is also the continuing tradition of personal immediacy. That is, both the housewife and the vendor take greater satisfaction in buying and selling a fresh article for whose quality both are responsible than in the exchange of something manufactured elsewhere, for whose quality no one is finally responsible.

To compare the color, the vivacity, the humane intercourse of either the large central markets or even the smaller specialty shops with the grim silence (punctuated by cash registers, underscored by Muzak) of a large supermarket is a primary lesson in the meaning of urbanity.

Barcelona was the first city in Spain to install a gas lighting system and, later, the first to introduce electricity. Gas lighting was tried experimentally in the courtyard of the stock exchange in 1826 and first used commercially to light the Paseo de Gracia (the extension of the Ramblas leading into the Ensanche) in 1854. Until very recently gaslights lined both the

Question: *Is it more fun to shop at individual stores (like this butcher on Calle de Martinez Anido) or at a supermarket? Do you prefer efficiency or human contact?*

lower and upper Ramblas. Few of them are still to be found, but the city continues to employ several dozen lamplighters who cart their ladders and wicks and cans of oil from lamppost to lamppost in certain areas. The soft glow of gas lamps in a public street, no matter what the cost in efficiency, is still preferable to the harsher glare of electric lighting; in fact, it has become a luxury reserved for the fanciest streets.

Electricity was introduced commercially in 1857 (only three years after gas) but city streets and private homes were not generally lighted by electricity until well after 1900. Electricity has always been a problem to Barcelona. Spinning turbines by steam requires the consumption of coal or fuel oil, and Spain has very little coal and almost no oil deposits. The coal sources of Asturias, for example, were all but exhausted by 1920, and the price of both soft and anthracite coal has steadily risen over the years. Fuel oil must be entirely imported from abroad. On the other hand, water-generated turbines require the damming and taming of rivers. But the only river large enough to produce sufficient electricity for Barcelona's needs within one hundred miles is the Ebro, spilling down from the Pyrenees in the north and west. It runs through narrow, high gorges, and its harnessing required a total, national effort. Such an effort was simply not forthcoming from the corrupt governments under the monarchy and was beyond the means of the Republic. Only since World War II has the Ebro finally been brought under control.

But today the demands for electricity on the Rio Ebro project have far outstripped its ability to produce. Furthermore, during the hot summer months, the river runs low and sometimes merely trickles. So electricity continues to be expensive in Barcelona—about four times the American kilowatt-hour rate; and in the summer, during certain hours of the day, there is no electricity at all except for essential services such as hospitals. There is no cheap or easy solution to Barcelona's power problem. Only the eventual construction of atomic power stations offers hope for the future. Yet, perversely, even the impersonal supply of gas and electricity contributes to a feeling of participation and civic solidarity—that of exasperation. Whether you are rich or poor, no matter where you live, the lights are bound to go out sooner or later. That feeling of a commonly shared disaster which on rare occasions (such as the great Northeast power failure of 1966) brings out a sense of urban fellowship in American cities is an almost daily occurrence in Barcelona.

Another daily occurrence, one which brings out feelings not of fellowship but of savagery, is the struggle to get from place to place in the city. Barcelona's public transportation problem will stand comparison with that of any city anywhere. There are buses (about 300 in daily circulation), electric buses (about 50), trolley lines (with about 225 clanging cars rattling over the tracks on any given day), and, of course, subways. The buses, which are single-decker and under the absolute authority of the ticket collector, not the driver, carry some 200,000,000 passenger fares per year. Simple arithmetic will give some idea of the desperation with which people must scramble for standing room on these vehicles (many stand on the platform, hanging on for dear life as the bus careens around corners).

*The leisurely pace of the Ramblas—not even disturbed by the subway entrance.*

The proportion of vehicles on the other lines—trolleys and electric buses—is not better. The trolleys carry 165,000,000 fares per year, the electric buses 25,000,000. Trolleys, noisy and street-blocking (they cannot get out of the way), are on their way out. By 1970 they will most probably have disappeared. This will save the city electricity (electric buses are also doomed) but rob it of some color. Deisel-powered buses are replacing the electric vehicles—to besmirch the atmosphere with their intolerable fumes and simply to add to Barcelona's fantastic traffic congestion. No good solution to the problem of surface transportation in Barcelona has yet been offered. Except for long distances, most people prefer to walk—it is quicker.

The Barcelona subway, which is clean, rapid and altogether too small for the city's needs, carries some 250,000,000 passengers through the bowels of the earth each year. Like subway systems at rush hours elsewhere in the world it is an inferno; great crowds of people shuffling resignedly forward to be stampeded, shoved and packed onto the overflowing platforms and bursting cars, the roaring and screaming of the trains, the demonic fury of the guards and conductors and ticket takers. All this is much the same as it is in New York, London or Paris. But in Barcelona, partly because the impersonality of the modern world arrived relatively late, partly because of the age-old temper of the people, individuals and crowds alike have not yet learned to anticipate the needs of the system. Waiting for subway trains, buses or trolleys, citizens of Barcelona do not fall naturally into queues with that docility displayed by Londoners or New Yorkers. There is a self-conscious feeling of humiliation to a Catalan in being treated (or treating himself) as an interchangeable unit within an impersonal system. Thus there is still hope that eventually he may escape or modify the system.

There are nine publicly supported hospitals in Barcelona; three of them entirely financed by the city, one partly financed by municipal authorities and partly by the bishopric, the rest part private, part provincially supported. They handle about seventy thousand patients a year and, though the buildings are old (many date from late medieval times, others from the nineteenth century; none are new), the standards of hygiene and of medicine are very high. Although lacking some of the more complex and expensive ultramodern equipment (the first cancer-therapy machine employing atomic isotopes was installed only in 1968), they make up in intimate, personal cheerfulness what they lack in efficiency—and that, too, is good medical practice.

There are 320 public primary schools in Barcelona, 20 of them municipal, the rest national; and more than 630 private or religious primary schools. This overwhelming discrepancy between public and private education reflects the fact that in Spain the Catholic Church (the official state religion) continues to control education, both directly through its parochial school system and indirectly through control of the programs and materials within the public school system. The more than 150,000 pupils in Barcelona's primary schools, whether they attend municipal, national or religious schools, spend a surprisingly large part of their time studying Biblical history and church dogma. Other subjects are taught primarily by rote, the entire class rising to recite in singsong fashion the multiplication tables, the kings of Spain, the capitals of foreign countries, and so on. Both subject matter and method are reminiscent of the American educational system of, say, 1890. All attempts to modernize either method or content run afoul of both religious and government suspicion. Children in Barcelona, as in the rest of Spain, are required to attend school until they reach the age of fourteen. New laws, not in effect until 1971, will keep them in school until they are sixteen. And this entire program of required education falls within the primary level (which includes, in later years, courses normally taught in high school in the United States). However, if, at the age of eleven or twelve, a child can pass the necessary examinations, he may then proceed with secondary-level education at one of the national institutes—and about sixty thousand children attend each year. The program of studies at the institute lasts six years, corresponding roughly to four years of American high school and the first two years of college, at the end of which graduates receive the baccalaureate degree. Their competence and acquired learning at this point is comparable to that of juniors in one of the better, or graduates of the average, American college.

Barcelona University, opened in 1539 under the patronage of the municipal Council of One Hundred, includes faculties of liberal arts, medicine, law, philosophy and science. Its buildings, which, with few exceptions, date from the nineteenth century, dominate the Plaza Universidad just off Plaza Cataluña on the edge of the Ensanche. About four thousand students attend the university, dividing their time, like students

*The uses of open space—Plaza Universidad*

elsewhere, between studies and riots. But there are more direct and personal reasons for Barcelona student riots than for many such which occur in other countries. For although the university is nominally free of both religious and governmental control, in actuality its courses of study, its materials and its entire program are heavily dominated by both. Students comparing the education they receive at Barcelona University with the education available to French or German or American university students are agonizingly aware that they are not being fitted or trained to the highest modern standards. Understandable resentment over this has steadily grown into resentment against the entire municipal and national regime which is ultimately responsible. Riots, police violence, the closing of various faculties from time to time by the government—all these have become serious symptoms of the malaise which runs all through the Spanish educational system and is especially obvious and irritating on its highest levels.

The police who might be called upon to deal with student disorders are many and varied in Barcelona. There are municipal police, devoted primarily to traffic control, various special provincial forces and the Guardia Civil—half police, half National Guard, heavily armed, organized in regular army formations and under national control. The relative position of the various Barcelona police establishments accurately reflects the relative power of the nation and the province in municipal affairs. All real power and authority rests with the Guardia Civil, responsible solely and directly to the Captain-General of Catalonia, who in turn is responsible solely and directly to the head of state,

General Francisco Franco. Felonies—grand larceny, murder, and so on—will be handled by special forces of the Guardia Civil, the Criminal Investigation Brigade. Trials for these offenses will be held in national, not municipal, courts; often enough they will be military courts-martial. But while the Guardia Civil and, through them, the national authorities, jealously guard their supreme power over the city, the municipal authorities, still consisting of the mayor, the Council of One Hundred, and various city commissions, are allowed through municipal police to handle the more common and vexing problems of city order, inspection and transportation. Misdemeanors such as petty theft, vagrancy, and so on are judged in municipal courts.

Barcelona never really regained the civic independence it lost during the late Renaissance. Democratic forms are still followed (after a twenty-year lapse at the end of the 1936–1939 civil war), but in themselves are not very meaningful. City councillors are elected, but the vote is restricted to heads of households or property holders. The mayor is elected by the Council of One Hundred but must be approved by the national authorities in Madrid. Membership on the highest organ of civic government is, in effect, limited to the rich, the conservative, the business community. All this could produce a much more restrictive government than it does. For the Barcelona ruling class—and under the circumstances of restricted voting and political opportunity it is fair to refer to it as a class—still finds itself at odds with the national government of Spain. There is, first of all, the separate Catalan cultural and historical heritage. Of greater immediate importance, however, is the fact that until very recently,

Catalonia (which is to say, primarily, Barcelona), as the greatest industrial center of Spain, felt itself over-taxed and underrepresented in national affairs. The rest of Spain, underdeveloped, agricultural and poor could not supply a market for Catalan manufactured goods. On the other hand, heavy export duties and centralized control of export policy prevented Catalan manufacturers from selling their goods abroad. To successfully resist (and from time to time they have been successful) national authority, the mercantile and manufacturing families who control Barcelona needed the support of all its people. Hence their administration of civic municipal affairs has been in fact, if not in theory, much more benevolent, progressive, lenient and civic-spirited than the municipal administrations of many cities under more purely democratic regimes.

But in recent years national conditions have changed dramatically. The Spanish gross national product has been increasing by a fantastic 6 per cent per year, the national economy has been enjoying an unprecedented boom and Spain now provides a more than sufficient market for Catalonian manufacturing. Coupled with this is the fact that the workers of Catalonia and Barcelona remain under the control of state-sponsored and state-controlled syndicates which take the place of trade unions but fulfill almost none of their functions. Strikes are barely tolerated, sometimes put down violently; the national social security system is under-financed, poorly administered and unable to cope with social needs; workers have little power, politically or economically. So while some of the grievances which have in the past united the citizens of Barcelona against the rest of Spain are disappearing, the inter-

*A new football (soccer) stadium on the city's outskirts—functional design, but dysfunctional new locus of traffic problems*

class grievances within the city itself have not been alleviated. This, given the stormy history of the city, does not bode well for the future. An accidental combination of various factors—general prosperity, the effective if remote authoritarianism of the national government, a still-vivid feeling of cultural apartness—has given the city an air of civic and social solidarity. It is very questionable if such a spirit can be maintained in the future.

Meanwhile, the business of Barcelona remains—business. The stately banks which huddle around the expanse of Plaza Cataluña represent a very real economic power. They hold more than forty billion pesetas in savings accounts ($5.7 billion) and continue to finance the activities of a stock exchange on which stocks to the value of four billion pesetas ($570 million) are traded annually. Their wealth is, of course, based on the manufacturing and commerce of the entire province of Catalonia, but of that Barcelona supplies a heavy share. The days when Barcelona's prosperity depended upon her maritime supremacy have long since vanished. The port now handles about 3,000 vessels a year, importing or exporting about four million tons of cargo and 30,000 passengers annually. But all the activity of the port, from ship construction to baggage transference, provides employment for only 20,000 people. More than 100,000 citizens of Barcelona are employed in metallurgical industries—steel mills, iron foundries and copper refining. Still more (about 180,-000) are employed in light industries (with textiles predominating). More than 120,000 are employed in commerce—buying and selling what their fellow citizens have made. It will be seen then that although the existence of the great port of Barcelona provided the vital magnet to attract industry and supply the capital necessary for the exploitation of natural resources, those same industries now completely dominate the economic life of the city.

As man does not live by bread alone, neither does a city. The metabolism of Barcelona is not simply the means whereby it feeds, lights, governs, educates and polices itself; it is also the metabolism of thought, culture and pleasure. If the city was once a place where men gathered to worship the gods or God, or to celebrate the Christian order on earth, it is, or ought to be, in its highest manifestation today, a place in which culture develops and from which it can be transmitted to other areas and to succeeding generations. Of course the very structure and existence of various large areas of Barcelona, especially the Gothic Quarter, imply the successful transmission of a cultural heritage. But there are more conscious and concentrated means whereby the city does that as well. There are, for example, the more than 1.7 million volumes (including some of the world's major collections of medieval manuscripts) to be found in its many libraries; there are the unsurpassed collections of pre-Renaissance and Romanesque carvings, wood paintings and tapestries to be found in such municipally financed museums as the Museo de Arte de Catalonia, the Museo Arqueologico and the Museo de Artes Decorativas; there is the brilliant collection of paintings to be found in the Museo de Arte Moderno, and the new collection of paintings by Pablo Picasso (an adopted son of Barcelona) now housed in a former palace in the Gothic Quarter; there are the marvelous specialized collec-

*The survival of handicraft—
carpenters making oars at a
small shop on the waterfront*

tions of maritime history, theatrical history and the history of the city of Barcelona—all housed in municipal museums, all open (free or at very modest admission prices) to the public. There are, too, the more than five thousand new titles brought out annually by Barcelona's book publishers (in spite of a haphazard national censorship), more than a thousand of which are in Catalan (the ban against that language was relaxed by the central government in 1956).

An interesting aspect of the preservation of such past cultural glories as the entire Gothic Quarter and various palaces and churches scattered around the city is the preservation of the crafts necessary for their upkeep. The filigree ironwork, the hand-painted tiles, the woven tapestries, the statuary, the illuminated altars that decorated an older Barcelona have been kept in a state of excellent repair and have even been replaced from time to time, thereby providing a market for skills no longer to be found in more modern cities. Narrow alleys near the port still ring from time to time with the blows of the blacksmith's hammer; carpentry shops can be found in which master craftsmen hand-hew wood. That these artisans (they grow fewer with passing decades) have lost none of the skill of their forefathers is proved by the fact that only experts can tell (and even they are sometimes mistaken) where ancient ironwork or tiling or carving ends and the new begins in many old buildings.

This then, in brief compass, is how the civic theater maintains itself, a glimpse backstage at the circuits and rigging, the machinery and economics of civic life. Out front, onstage, an ageless urban drama continues, seeking new forms with passing years.

# 5 The Modern Stage Becoming

*God is merciful, and He inspired the Generation
of '98 to say: "Enough of straight lines!"*

—CARLOS SOLDEVILA

But like many prophets, those of the Generation of
'98 were long without honor in their own land. The
"Generation"—meaning the writers, philosophers, po-
ets and artists who came to maturity around the turn
of the present century—was named for the year in
which Spain lost the last of her overseas empire to an
expansionist United States. That defeat, supposedly,
by revealing the bankruptcy of political life in Spain,
shocked the new generation into progressive thought.
But it was to be only after many decades and much
bloodshed that the new thought was to find expression
in steel and concrete and the layout of city streets.

First, as we have seen, the inherent warfare of the
socio-civic jungle had to erupt and fight itself out dur-

*Gaudí's Güell Park is a triumph of useful fantasy, functional imagination.*

ing the Civil War of 1936-1939. At the end of that war traditionalist Spain, the victor, tried to stop the clock of social progress. Aided by Spain's isolation during World War II and subsequent years, the authoritarian government in Madrid was fairly successful in this. But sometime during the late 1950's the clock started ticking again—in Barcelona as throughout Spain. And with political passions burned out, proscribed and widely suspect, the people of Barcelona turned for inspiration to their own cultural heritage, fortunately preserved throughout all the centuries of social disintegration. The future was to be based, not on the idea of class warfare or urban exploitation, but on an attempt to rediscover and express those civic and architectural factors making for integration.

Part of Barcelona's cultural heritage has always been a willingness to look outward, to consider the city as part of a general European-Mediterranean culture, to receive ideas from abroad. The new sections of the city which were to arise in recent decades made full use of city planning and architectural ideas derived from foreign sources. In the new buildings one could see the styles of Frank Lloyd Wright, Le Corbusier, Mies van der Rohe markedly adapted to Barcelona's particular needs. One could discover the idea of shopping and civic malls, derived from the rebuilding of Amsterdam, finding expression in the new outlying districts of the city. Above all, one could sense the influence of Barcelona's own flourishing Gothic period, expressed in modern ways.

Physically, the new Barcelona grew (and is still growing) in the areas beyond the Ensanche, west and southwest of the nineteenth century city. As early as

1914 the former towns of Sans, San Gervasio, Gracia, San Andres, San Martin, Horta and Sarria had been officially incorporated into the expanding city. The areas between these towns and between them all and the older city remained largely vacant, however, until very recent times. Only the suburban houses of the rich rose amid the ample fields, and a few monasteries. But the existence of these residences, as well as the existence of the older towns which were incorporated, was a stroke of great fortune for the city. For the suburban houses of the rich were often excellent expressions of nineteenth century architectural forms, while the old towns retained even older street plans. In other words, as modern Barcelona expanded outward, it was forced to incorporate a variety of urban styles dating from as early as the eleventh century (in the case of Sarria). The new roads and boulevards which were to enmesh the new districts as often as not came to an abrupt end at a Renaissance marketplace or before (in Pedralbes) the majestic towers of a medieval monastery. Even if Barcelona's twentieth century architects and planners had wanted to impose the dreary order of a grid pattern on the new sections of the city, they could not have done so. But they did not want to. The lesson of the Ensanche had been quite enough: "No more straight lines!"

So the boulevards and avenues leading out to and between the ex-towns, although wide enough to accommodate modern traffic needs, do not generally run in straight lines. They curve gently, following natural contours in the land. They give way often enough to eccentrically shaped plazas, lose themselves in the maze of medieval streets of such ex-towns as Horta and

San Gervasio. And central garden-malls, fit for strolling, bisect many of them. Ample provision has also been made for trees and gardens and fountains and statues—all the artistic and decorative details which the citizens of Barcelona have come to expect as their civic and social right.

The older suburban houses of the rich were not, for the most part, torn down. And their presence created implicit problems for the architects of new private homes or apartment houses. There was no legal problem; architects could well have simply ignored the older structures (very often given over since 1936 to religious institutions, schools or other public enterprises), building around them in such a way as to hide, dwarf and eventually crowd them out of existence. But the new spirit of building was to preserve that which was of human interest from the past (and the gingerbread Victorian mansions *were* of human interest). So the new buildings maintained a respectful distance from the old and, where possible, were designed so as not to clash too violently in style and size.

As in other cities, by mid twentieth century, land in Barcelona had become so expensive that the building of new private homes became all but impossible—only high-rise apartment buildings could bring a worthwhile return to real estate investors. But in Barcelona, "high-rise" means about eight stories high. There are not more than a handful of buildings anywhere within or near the city that rise higher, none above twelve stories. Nor are the new apartment buildings and apartment-building developments the gray monoliths or huddle of prison-like structures familiar to New Yorkers, Chicagoans or Londoners. The buildings are

*And why not use pedestrian malls as open-air markets—especially for flowers and (as here on the Ramblas) brilliantly colored birds? Can there really be too much color in a city-scape?*

splashes of color. Where aluminum panels have been used, these are colored—bright red, bright blue, even orange or yellow. Massive use has been made of regional materials, such as tiles for outer décor. Balconies (almost every apartment in all the new buildings has a large balcony) are decorated by designs in colorful tile. Where concrete has been used it is most often decorated by stone-etched designs or figures, often colored also. The grounds around the new buildings are not parking lots, nor are they vast fields of grass; they are gardens, planned to be colorful year-round.

Barcelona architects and city planners have also avoided the construction of shopping centers in the new areas. An apartment building may have stores on its ground floor, and a line of such buildings on an avenue, providing stores and cafés and restaurants and cinemas, transforms that street into a shopping district for residents. But shopping is kept *in the street*, not segregated either to invade residential garden areas or to form wholly commercial enclaves around parking lots. Shopping is recognized, in other words, as a social affair, and the street is maintained as a general meeting place.

It will be seen, then, that Barcelona's outward expansion has been *urban*. The emphasis has been on urbanizing outlying districts, not on suburbanizing them. Barcelona, as it expands, remains Barcelona—it does not dribble away into a no man's land between city and country as do so many great modern cities. The all but indefinable feeling of urbanity, of being present in the city, with all it implies for the pace of social, intellectual and civic life, is as vivid on the outskirts as in the center.

If Barcelona has been strikingly successful in its urban expansion and its new building, not a little of the credit must be given to the plans, rules and co-ordinating influence of its Provincial Council of Urbanism, Architecture and Housing. Created by act of the central Madrid government in 1945, the Provincial Council has authority over all building and planning both within the city (from the Gothic Quarter to the farthest outer limit) and the entire Barcelona region. The power of the council is so great that its existence could probably only have come about under the authoritarian type of government which has dominated the country since 1939. Yet whatever its antecedents, the council has used its power in remarkably discreet, forward-looking and humane ways.

For purposes of planning and building regulations, Barcelona and its immediate environs are divided into eighteen zones. Each has its own architectural and planning rules especially adapted to its possibilities and needs.

The first zone comprises the old Gothic Quarter. Within this zone any new building must maintain, in height, distance from the street, design and decoration, the traditional forms of the largely medieval buildings around it. Only the smallest private shops, religious or cultural institutions are permitted. Of course, so much of the Gothic Quarter is made up of national, civic and religious monuments that there is hardly room for new building of any kind. And it might be thought that where new building was possible, the fact that it had to settle comfortably into the Gothic architecture of the whole quarter might make it all but impossible. But a striking example of how modern architecture can accommodate itself unobtrusively and gracefully to older forms has been the construction (within the last two years) of the new Picasso-decorated College of Architects—not fifty yards from the old cathedral. Although built of glass and aluminum and boldly decorated and colored, the College of Architects preserves the inner spirit of a Renaissance structure. So well does it fit into the architecture of the district that it is almost unnoticeable.

Zones two, three and four of the Provincial Council's plan encompass the primary commercial and shopping districts, such as the Ramblas, the older residential quarters around them and the nineteenth century Ensanche. Rules for new construction in these zones have the same intention as the rule promulgated for the Gothic Quarter—the general character of the districts is to be maintained, new buildings may not be built within them that do not correspond to the older architecture in size, volume and general appearance. The emphasis is on preservation.

Zones five, six and seven (which overlap certain earlier zones and each other) are defined as "semi-intensive," "intensive" and "extensive" residential zones. In the semi-intensive residential zone no more than 150 residential units per acre are permitted; in the intensive residential zone, 200 per acre; and in the extensive zone, no more than 100 per acre. This low density of population permitted in residential *urban* zones would, in such a city as New York or London or Paris, make these zones into all but suburbs. Furthermore, buildings in any of these zones may not occupy more than 30 per cent of the land on which they rest, and their height is limited to eight stories above the ground floor.

Industrial building is strictly prohibited in these zones, and commerce is restricted to the shops (to be incorporated within the residential blocks) necessary for the daily needs of the inhabitants. The architectural norms for new buildings are established for general areas (they vary widely in size and shape according to the topography of the ground and the existence of older structures), and any individual building within such an area must fit into the overall pattern of design and decoration.

Zones seven, eight and nine in the council plan are described as intensive to extensive garden city areas. But the use of the words "garden city" may be misleading to those familiar with the garden city proposals and plans long sponsored by city planners in the United States and England. The idea of the garden city was, supposedly, to relieve urban congestion and bring the countryside back into urban life by building self-contained urban centers beyond the city, protected from its encroachments by open countryside or "green belts." This is, in fact, an attack upon urbanism, an attack upon the very nature and character of the city—a flight from the city. But the garden city areas encompassed within the Barcelona plan spring from no such intention, but rather its opposite. They are thought of as new areas of urbanization, not of de-urbanization. Thus the buildings in these zones are required to fill as much as 40 per cent of the land on which they are built; their street fronts must be more than twelve yards wide. Light industry is encouraged, as are street shops. Shopping centers are forbidden and apartment houses and hotels must provide, within themselves, sufficient parking space for at least 50 per cent of the

*New housing on the city's outskirts continues the essentially urban patterns of city life. No catering to suburbia here.*

number of people inhabiting the structure. Private houses are permitted, but the sizes of plots (varying from one hundred to five hundred square yards) are such as to make the land cost all but prohibitive for this use. Once again, within these zones, although more freedom of architectural variation is permitted, all new buildings must be approved by the council's architects on the basis of their harmonizing with the general architectural character of the zone.

Other zones (especially numbers fifteen and eighteen) are devoted to the establishment and protection of parks and green belts. Aside from those parks already incorporated in the city, an additional twelve parks are planned within the newly built-up areas. Building within them is absolutely prohibited, except for (in the case of the new large "natural parks") geological or botanical gardens and laboratories, and in certain cases, public recreational structures. It is notable, however, that at least one municipally owned (though privately managed) outdoor café is permitted in each park. The rules for use of public parks in Barcelona are far less rigorous than they are, for example, in London. Private portable radios and phonographs are permitted (largely because until very recently there were but few of them in Barcelona), though a campaign is currently under way to ban them. There are no "keep off the grass" signs, nor are there fences. On the other hand, there is very little grass. Grass requires an enormous amount of water, and Barcelona's relatively dry climate and the scarcity of irrigation water limits the amount that may be grown. On the other hand, Barcelona parks are riots of subtropical gardening. Cactuses of every kind, exotic (to northern eyes) flowers and shrubs, palm trees abound everywhere. And unlike the parks in, say, New York or Los Angeles, there is almost no littering problem, although few litter baskets are to be seen, and the people of the city use their parks at least as intensively as the people of any other city. It seems that hundreds of generations of continuous residence amid historic monuments, beautiful plazas and streets, has finally bred a citizen so conscious of his environment as a continuing work of art that he normally disciplines himself against abusing it.

The Provincial Council's control over present and future building is expressed through a licensing system administered by the municipal government of Barcelona. Licenses to build, demolish or alter (in however minute a way) must be obtained from the city government, and they are granted only after they have been approved by the City-Provincial Technical Commission, including architects, engineers, public sanitation experts and others. Penalties are severe, including fines and prison sentences.

Given the authoritarian nature of the government, planning and enforcement of rules regarding new construction are relatively easy. Not so easy is the enforcement of rigorous standards of sanitation, hygiene and architectural taste amid the old slums of Barcelona. A law passed in 1944 to deal with all housing in the Barcelona area was, sensibly (and hopefully), made retroactive in its application. That is, the norms established for new housing were automatically to be enforced against old, too. Some of the rules are instructive. For example, all family dwelling units have to have a minimum of kitchen-dining room combination, private bathroom and bedroom large enough for two beds. Each room has to be independent, none serving as a passageway to any other, and each has to have a window for direct lighting and ventilation. Double bedrooms have to be a minimum of ten square meters (about 11 square yards) in area; all ceilings have to be at least two and one half yards high. These rules are instructive because, applied as they were to *all* housing in Barcelona, they automatically made illegal the slum housing of such districts as the Chinese Quarter and Barceloneta. The application of the new laws, and their interpretation, has produced in Barcelona something new in ways to attack the crisis of central city slums that afflicts so many modern cities.

In London, slum clearing was accomplished (haphazardly) by German bombing raids during World War II, and certain feeble efforts on the part of the county council since that time. In New York and other American cities, slum clearance is generally accomplished by municipal condemnation proceedings. In both cases, the idea has been to raze, completely, to absolutely clear out all the old buildings and then construct an entirely new (generally high-rise) complex of housing units. But a neighborhood is more than its buildings, however decayed they may be. In fact a neighborhood is an organism almost as complex as a human body. It cannot be renewed by obliterating it. The infinitely varied and complicated threads of social, commercial and human relationships that form the living web of a neighborhood, when brushed away, can never be reestablished. Even less drastic surgery than clearing the entire area may lead to inflicting mortal wounds; as, for example, the driving through a neigh-

*Nothing super-human disrupts the neighborhood pattern.*

borhood of a highway that cuts it in two, or the building of a skyscraper which, by heavily overconcentrating residents, turns the neighborhood into one vast parking lot.

Too often in American cities slum clearance has not actually meant the rehousing of the poor within the same area; it has represented a grab at desirable land by wealthier elements of the population and the dispersal of the poor to other slum areas in the city. But, even when the same inhabitants are returned to the same area, housed now in the the high-rise housing developments, the neighborhood has been effectively destroyed. The rigorous application of zoning rules which banishes the small shops, the saloons, the narrow streets—in short, the social nucleii of the poor inhabitants—banishes also their entire feeling of local unity, the atmosphere of neighborliness, even, in many cases the physical possibilities of simply meeting their friends.

Barcelona, in handling the problem of older city slums, did not clear them away (natural demolition, the destruction of buildings grown through age too dangerous for habitation, always goes on, of course). The reasons for this heretical attitude were varied and partly accidental. First of all, after the exhaustions and disasters of the civil war, followed by the restrictions of the Second World War (in which, although Spain was neutral, it suffered economically), there simply wasn't the money or resources available to engage in sweeping slum-clearance programs. Besides that, the lack of resources and attention devoted to city planning during the decades of war had resulted in an acute housing shortage which saw thousands of people living in caves and shanties on Barcelona's outskirts. Social pressures were such that to destroy existing housing, thereby forcing thousands more into such habitations for the several years new construction would have required, might well have led to a social explosion. And too, the people of Barcelona, living within the continuing historic matrix represented by the older sections of the city, were very wary of destroying anything at all.

So slum clearance was not accomplished by bulldozers but by law. The overcrowding which is the very core of slum definition, was made illegal. Landlords were forced to evict the people they had been gouging by crowding them into small apartments, sometimes three families to a room. These people were then housed in new municipal-private developments within the semi-intensive, or garden-city zones away from the city's core. But it must be remembered that city planners in Barcelona have maintained urban concentration in these zones, given them a city-neighborhood character. So those removed to them were not set adrift suddenly on a sea of suburban or rural life. Their city habits of thought and behavior found fully adequate means of fulfillment in their new surroundings. On the other hand, the jointly financed (municipal-private) new housing was a long time in completion. Many thousands suffered hardship, many were forced to emigrate to other cities. Once again, probably only the authoritarian nature of the national regime made the wave of expulsions possible.

With the lightening of the strain of overcrowding, regulations regarding sanitary and hygienic minimums for housing were strictly enforced, thereby requiring

*New construction has been truly integrated into the former slum of Barceloneta—without damaging the neighborhood as an organism.*

the slumlords either to expend the necessary money to light, ventilate and refurbish their buildings or face fines and jail sentences or sell their holdings to someone who would comply with the law. But structural changes in slum buildings, insofar as they affected the outer appearance of individual structures and the harmony of the entire area, were approached with great care. In Barceloneta it was found necessary to demolish and reconstruct buildings over about 10 per cent of the area. But the new buildings were of the same height and dimensions as the old, were built of the same outer materials and were styled to harmonize with existing structures. Repairs to the structure and façades of the old buildings were carefully controlled so as to maintain the same appearance and harmonies. The small shops and cafés and little commercial enterprises (carpenters, blacksmiths, garages, and so on) were not zoned out of the area; they were simply, like everyone else, required to maintain the new building standards.

The result has been (the program is not yet finished —there are still blights throughout the area) something new in the way of slum clearance. The slum has not, in fact, been "cleared." It has been abolished in a social and human sense. The people living there are still poor, and neither the area nor the individual living units are attractive to higher-income groups. But Barceloneta can no longer be considered a slum in any meaningful definition of the word. Overcrowding no longer exists, decent standards of sanitation and hygiene are enforced; where structural changes or alterations have been necessary they have been made. And the area is almost untouched as a neighborhood. It has maintained without a break its historic continuity as a local environment; its friendships, customs, small commercial relationships—these are untouched and as flourishing as ever. And all this may provide a most important lesson to city planners elsewhere in the world.

One final observation may be made. Barceloneta, it will be recalled, was built as a workers' barracks quarter. Its housing and buildings were something new and ugly imposed on the former Gothic order of Barcelona. Yet today, these workers' barracks (cleared, as has been pointed out above) are infinitely more attractive than the monolithic best that city housing authorities have provided in other major cities. No more devastating commentary on the lack of imagination and honest social intentions of urban planners in the modern world could possibly be made.

If slum transformation was effected in Barceloneta by the strict application of zoning and sanitation laws as well as the imposition of heavy municipal pressure, the attack on another central city slum, that of the old Chinese Quarter, has taken the form of a strictly hands-off policy. Once again, it is hard to say exactly what the final intentions of the Provincial Council and the municipal authorities may have been, though the effect is apparent. In the Chinese Quarter, laws of hygiene and sanitation, rules for the protection of private housing were simply not enforced. The result has been that this land, right off the central Ramblas, much more valuable commercially than residentially, has risen in price to the point where residential use is all but prohibitive—and nonexistent. Landlords can no longer afford to use their land or the buildings on it

Traffic (as in this Barrio Chino street)
is the great enemy of the sense of locality—
and even of the physical existence of
neighborhoods.

for slums. More importantly, the city has in no way interfered (it has tacitly encouraged) their using it for commercial purposes, despite older zoning statutes. Thus the whole quarter has slowly been converted into a maze of night clubs, bars, cafés, restaurants—and shops, warehouses and very small manufacturing units. In other words, rather than attempting to make use of this central-city land for residential purposes, it has been allowed to take its natural course into fully commercial usage. This too is a unique, if ironic, way to clear a "slum."

It has its uses. The Chinese Quarter has rapidly become a combination Times Square–State Street–Soho area, an entertainment region right in the heart of the city, easily reachable, maintaining some of the desperate charm of its old and decrepit atmosphere, illuminated now by neon and flashing lights. Of course vice and crime flourish here (there is relatively little violence, but much vice in Barcelona), but in a sense they are also isolated, if concentrated, in the area. Writers on Barcelona have spoken with real pride of the fact that as a center of notoriety, danger (mostly imaginary) and the less innocent diversions of mankind, the Chinese Quarter can stand comparison with the worst that any city in the world has to offer. In essence, the possibility of all-but-purposely creating a Chinese Quarter is based on the very ancient civic-human consciousness of a very ancient city. Neither the citizens nor the municipal government of Barcelona entertain many illusions about human nature after two thousand years' experience with it. Perhaps it seems natural to them to provide an outlet for some of its more instinctive aspects. In any event, the ancient street layout, the small old buildings, the shady atmosphere of the quarter make it a natural Disneyland of wickedness—human, not inhuman, wickedness—and as such it is delightful.

In contemplating Barcelona's modern stage, we have stressed some of its positive aspects. There are negative ones also, which will be examined later. But here it might be well to point out that what is most attractive in the new Barcelona-becoming is directly attributable to the city's past, is an organic growth from it, both physically and socially. The reason that new apartment buildings are colorful rather than drab is because the people of Barcelona demand color and art in their surroundings. They demand these things because they have always had them—from medieval times, despite the eighteenth–nineteenth century hiatus. The reason why no new structures rise more than eight or nine stories in the city or on its outskirts is because the people of Barcelona would not approve. They would not approve because they have always considered themselves as supreme in their environment, not abstract symbols of power. If their city is to be exploited at all, it is to be exploited as a human and humane environment, a continuing stage for their performance of a life drama.

And very much of this feeling for the city is quite conscious and self-aware. It has preserved several expressions of civic life which have vanished from almost all other great modern cities. If we have insisted on the physical stage upon which this life drama takes place, let's see if we can identify some basic human expressions of civic life which arise naturally from the urban environment and, in turn, ensure its continuity.

# 6 An Urban Life

*Catalans, you are children; you are drowning in aesthetics!*
—MIGUEL DE UNAMUNO

Which is something of an exaggeration. As consciously as the citizens of Barcelona have surrounded their lives with art, very few could be said to be going down for the third time in it. Yet there is something to be said for the attempt to inform life, even amid the clamor of the modern world, with dramatic purpose and what grace can be snatched from necessity. And Barcelonians of all classes do make such an attempt.

Take, for example, the question of ritual. All human societies of any worth have prized ritual, both private and public. It provides a sense of order; supplies a conscious link with past ways and customs; subordinates individual problems within a social context; provides a touch of glamor and art to humdrum activities. But it must, of course, be meaningful. A ritual whose personal or social content has disappeared becomes an act of self-mockery, destructive of human pride. Ritual which is still expressive of real human needs and emotions can lend an immense dignity to life; ritual which has become mere spectacle can degrade that same life. So great is the human need for ritual that in those places (such as the United States) where ancient and medieval rites and customs are not part of the national heritage, ritual is constantly being invented—and the more gaudy, solemn and ornate it is, the better. One thinks of the rites and rituals of such organizations as the Elks, the Shriners, the Odd Fellows, with all their glitter and sparkle and secrets. Empty as they are of any historical or real social content, they obviously fill a need among their thousands of devotees. But the citizen of Barcelona has no need to invent ritual; his life is permeated with it, and most of it is very meaningful indeed.

Most ritual in Barcelona (as in other Latin capitals) is, of course, religious, the surviving heritage of medieval Christian social function. It makes little difference whether the individual still believes in the Catholic religion or its functionaries. Such occasions as births, marriages, baptisms, communions and deaths are celebrated almost universally throughout the city as very important family (and social) holidays. But they are more than *fiestas*—they are solemn historical rituals, expressions of age-old custom. A baptism, for example, must be celebrated by a banquet thrown by the parents, at no matter what personal or financial cost. To omit it would be unthinkable. A first communion also calls for a banquet, but, of more importance to the communicant, it demands that she or he wear the appropriate costume for the occasion—a bridal dress for girls, formal attire for boys. Most first communions occur at the age of nine, so the children of Barcelona, from that very early age, have participated in formal, socially sanctified, socially meaningful and ornate ceremony. Of course, despite the innumerable friends who may be invited to attend these rituals, they are basically private in nature. But the permeation of private lives with ritual leads to the more natural acceptance of public ritual.

The Good Friday processions which take place in every Spanish town or city, and are celebrated magnificently in Barcelona, are examples. These are parades involving the city's civic leaders (the mayor and the Council of One Hundred as well as the provincial governor), the armed forces (Army bands supply the slow, dirgelike music), the city's religious leaders (including all the bishops and most of the lower clergy), the city's leading businessmen, and hundreds of plain citizens who feel moved to join the procession. Originally the Good Friday procession was intended to illustrate, in graphic play-form, the suffering and execution of Christ to a people who were illiterate and could not read their Bible (which was, in any case, in Latin). The procession, with citizens carrying statues of Christ and Mary and Joseph, and shoulder-born floats illustrating such scenes as the Last Supper, the Crucifixion, the Roman legionnaire offering a sponge of vinegar to the suffering Christ, made apparent and vivid a lesson that most people knew only from the words spoken in pulpits.

Today, of course, the instructive function of the

*Civic ritual lends dignity and grace to individual and community life—Barcelona is lucky to have a rich heritage.*

procession is no longer significant. But its historical ritual is. Not only are statues and floats carried through the streets, but men dressed as Roman legionnaires accompany them, and the whole procession is sprinkled by bands of people dressed in the outlandish costumes (like colored Ku Klux Klan outfits) of medieval penitents. In other words, the pageant has become not only a reminder of Biblical happenings but also of the way in which such happenings were illustrated in medieval times and of the unity of medieval faith. Although thousands march in these processions, most citizens watch from the sidelines in respectful silence. But the sense of total civic participation is maintained by those individuals moved to sing *saetas* (spontaneous religious songs) amid the crowds of onlookers. When a man suddenly falls to his knees on the sidewalk or a woman's voice is raised in shrill, Arab-like keening from a balcony, the entire procession comes to a halt until the *saeta* is finished. That is to say, all the great men of the city—its leaders in every walk of life, and the Army and all the clergy—stop and listen to the voice of an unknown participant whose right to demand their attention is unquestioned.

A more joyous religious-civic ritual is that which takes place on the twelfth night after Christmas. Spaniards, with somewhat more logic than others, do not give gifts on Christmas, which is kept as a solemn religious occasion. Instead, they give presents on the Day of the Three Kings—twelve days later, when, according to the legend, the three wise men presented their gold, frankincense and myrrh to the infant Jesus. Once again the city puts on a show—this time the arrival (by boat in the harbor accompanied by searchlights, screaming ship whistles and rockets) of the Three Kings, gorgeously dressed, riding camels and accompanied by a large retinue of Oriental guards and followers. The Three Kings parade throughout the city, to the delight of the children (and their parents), who line the route by the thousands. The parade (unlike the pre-Christmas sales parades which celebrate the arrival of Santa Claus in some American cities on Thanksgiving Day) is strictly noncommercial. No advertising is permitted or intended. It is entirely in the hands of the city itself and is celebrated as a civic, not a commercial, function. The Three Kings, arriving at various districts of the city, find already-piled-up gifts in local squares, which they then proceed to hand out to the crowds of expectant children. Santa Claus is a charming but *privately* motivated individual. He brings his gifts to private homes in secrecy. But the Three Kings, with all the excitement and glamor that an entire city can put into the occasion, distribute their gifts publicly, openly. A northern Christmas Day is an essentially private affair—the Day of the Three Kings is a social-civic celebration.

Another religious festival which has become almost entirely civic is that of St. John's Eve (June 24). Older than Christianity, the celebration has its roots in the pagan midsummer festivals. It is the occasion of building fires and driving out evil spirits. Various districts and streets in Barcelona compete with each other to create the most original, ornate and impressive wood-and-straw figures of the Devil and his lieutenants. These are erected (with infinite work and care involving all the neighbors) in various squares and plazas and, at midnight, are set afire. Many of these figures are two or three stories high, all are very carefully painted and clothed, and most have hidden fireworks within, so that when the flames reach them they shoot rockets out of their head or their eyes turn into fiery pinwheels. The religious significance of driving away evil spirits or burning the Devil has long since completely vanished from the St. John celebrations. But the construction of the figures, involving hundreds of citizens of each district or street, the burning of them (at which thousands gather to sing, drink and dance in the streets) and the interdistrict competition for the most impressive or grotesque of the figures provides yet another public-civic occasion in which practically all the people of Barcelona participate.

Participation is the key word. A parade at which the citizens of a city are carefully kept behind police barricades and are, in any event, prepared only to watch may be a civic demonstration—but it is not a civic celebration without the active participation of the people. It may amuse or inspire awe (most parades are, of course, military), but it cannot give people an inner sense of communality, of participating equally with all their fellow citizens in commonly shared joys and responsibilities. And unless such a feeling of participation is present, civic occasions are meaningless shows.

City-wide ritual-celebrations in Barcelona are supplemented by more local neighborhood festivals. Every city district has its own patron saint, and the saint's "feast day" is an occasion for public rejoicing, dancing in the streets, and so on. The district offers "open house" to all the people of the city (yes, and a certain amount of free food and drink as well as the neighborhood band to play for the dancing). As in the St.

John's celebrations, the religious overtones of a patron saint have all but completely vanished, the formerly religious has become a strictly social-civic ritual.

Not only privately, but publicly, almost every citizen of Barcelona has and continues to participate in ritual —the formalized drama, set on an urban stage, which not only provides him with occasions of merriment or of personal dignity, but also with a very real and deep sense of historical continuity, civic participation and public commitment. It may be said that Barcelona is simply lucky in having very ancient pagan-Christian-medieval rites and symbols worth celebrating. But other cities have as long a history—like London or Paris—yet do not provide their citizens with set-piece urban dramas to perform. The reason for this may be primarily that other cities, such as London or Paris, emerged much earlier into the modern industrial-capitalist world than did Barcelona. Not only the physical appurtenances of that world, in the shape of industry and skyscrapers, for example, but also the mental characteristics of it, have long since fragmented society and drowned ritual in such cities. Barcelona, though modern in a very full sense of the word, received both the blessings and curses of industrialization, capitalistic organization and irreligiosity relatively late in its career. Older modes of thought and behavior had not yet vanished. Also, having the sad experience of other cities to draw upon, Barcelona, but recently arrived in modern society, has been most wary about discarding earlier values. Furthermore, the extreme fragmentation of paleotechnic Barcelona, which led to bloody insurrection and civil war, was, after all, won in the end by traditionalist forces, forces determined to slow

*What to do with those three hours of rest at midday? Have a drink, talk to friends, eat a lunch made up of different snacks—relax.*

down the clock of social history and to preserve at least the outward forms of traditional behavior. Insofar as these forces (represented by the authoritarian central government in Madrid and its allies in the Church, the military and among the rich) have succeeded in preserving certain traditional values (even at terrible expense to the modern needs of the people), their victory has not been a total loss to the city.

If a city's attitude toward ritual is a key to understanding its life, its sense of time is the very rhythm of its life and a very sure measure of its success as an environment. Of course, it is to be expected that there is more hustle in a city, any city, than in a drowsy country crossroads town. The bringing together of very large numbers of people, increasing the "accidents of human encounter" which are among a city's chief functions, concentration of business and industry —all this makes for a faster-paced life. But when the pace of life increases to a superhuman tempo, bringing tensions to crisis point in the human (and perhaps it would be fair to say the city's) nervous system, then there is something basically wrong. To be under a social or an inner compulsion regarding time is as restrictive and inhumane as to be under any other kind of compulsion.

The citizens of Barcelona (like the people of Spain generally) are under absolutely no time compulsion. They are, at times, in a hurry—to get to work, to get to the movies, to meet a friend—but there is no social or discernible inner need for them to do so "on time." People are expected to be on time at their jobs, but very few commercial or industrial enterprises penalize the worker who is ten or fifteen minutes late. It would mean penalizing the entire staff daily. Nor do business-men or the owners of various enterprises make a fetish out of punctuality. There are at least as many tradi-tionally "self-made" business leaders in Barcelona as in, say, Chicago or New York, but they never ascribe their success to punctuality as did so many American businessmen in days gone by. Nor do their clients and customers expect excessive punctuality in the delivery of goods and services. When something is to be deliv-ered somewhere, it is customary for the buyer to ask if it will be delivered (if it is supposed to be) *mañana*. The seller generally agrees that it will. Then the cus-tomer must ask, *seguro* (surely)? In which case the seller will either shrug (meaning "No"), or he will say, "*Seguro, seguro,*" meaning that it really will be deliv-ered tomorrow. If the buyer does not inquire, or if the seller refuses to pronounce the double affirmative, delivery may be made any time during the next week or two. Or even later. But although this may lead to exasperated telephone calls, it almost never arouses deep or real resentment. Punctuality is not considered indispensable for business transactions. In other words, in Barcelona, time is not money. Someone who considered it to be so would be looked upon with very real pity or scorn by his fellow citizens.

Punctuality in social matters is considered almost rude. When you are invited to visit a Barcelona home you are expected, in the normal course of events, to be at least half an hour late. To arrive on time would be to impose on the hosts. Likewise, appointments made to meet in public places are made with the under-standing that there must be at least a half hour leeway. In a city with easily available parks, innumerable plazas and squares, and many hundreds of outdoor cafés, this is entirely possible. It is a far different matter to allow someone to wait half an hour on a windy, traffic-infested street corner with no place to sit and no means of passing the time than to allow him to sit over a drink at a café table, watching the world pass by as he waits for you.

The business day in Barcelona (and the school day) starts officially at nine o'clock in the morning. Many industrial enterprises begin work at eight, and many shops do not open until nine-thirty or ten. Traditionally, ten o'clock was opening time, but this is slowly changing. Shops and businesses stay open until one-thirty or two (increasingly, nowadays, they stay open only until one. There follows a three-hour period devoted to lunch, rest and conviviality. The city opens again for business at 4:00 P.M. and continues work until eight or eight-thirty. Traditionally, the long noon-time *siesta* hour has been ascribed to the excessive heat of the Mediterranean day. But in the case of Barcelona this is patently false. The climate is not even sub-tropical. While most days are sunny, autumn days are cool and winter days are cold. Nor does the temperature during spring and summer generally rise to the climax of Denver or Detroit. Barcelona's weather is definitely temperate, comparable perhaps to that of Richmond, Virginia.

What, then, is the significance of the long lunch hour? Basically, it is symbolic of the fact that in Barcelona time is not something to be exploited but to be enjoyed. It is assumed that a person needs more than an hour to consume and digest a meal, that a person requires more than an hour of relaxation in the middle of the business or industrial day. It is even assumed that he may want to spend some time at home at midday. Whatever his desire in this respect, it would occur to no one to infringe on his most basic human right—that of passing his time as he sees fit. In practice, the three-hour midday break generally means that a person spends about half an hour in travel to and from the job, about an hour sitting at a café with his friends chatting, and another hour and a half in a restaurant eating a leisurely lunch. Or he may have his leisurely lunch at home, or in a park, or sitting on a wharf. All this provides him not only with much-needed relaxation but also with an opportunity to enjoy (most of the year) the outdoors during the most pleasant part of the day.

The absence of time compulsion makes a dramatic difference in the atmosphere of a city. Some people, of course, are in a hurry at any given moment, but most are not. The pace of pedestrian traffic on the streets is very slow compared to any American city. And when people are not in a hurry, they have more time to notice the details of their environment and to enjoy them. A building façade, a statue in a park, the garden of a plaza or a fountain—these become intimate friends. Plans advanced to remove or destroy buildings, plazas and streets in the interest of greater efficiency meet a very real and deeply personal opposition from people who have the time to become intimately acquainted with them. Leisure, in other words, becomes a very weighty factor in practical civic planning. Likewise, the construction of new buildings, or the opening of new streets or plazas, must take account of the fact that people will be strolling down them

*The life of the street need not be
hurried, nerve wracking, anti-human.*

slowly with an eye out for the décor of their environment. The building that presents a blank façade of glass and aluminum, the street that is not properly lined with trees and bisected with gardens, the plaza that is not centered around a fountain or a garden, the area which does not provide plenty of pleasant sitting space is received with ridicule and indignation by the citizens of Barcelona, and generally effectively prevented.

And it is instructive to note that despite (or, perhaps, because of) the relatively slower pace of Barcelona life, the relaxed attitude of its people, the lack of time compulsion—everything that has to be done gets done. It seems that punctuality, hurry and rush are not, after all, essential to the efficient operation of commerce and industry, as the city's prosperity and skyrocketing production index reveal.

A sense of ritual, the pace of time—and there is yet another important aspect of daily life in Barcelona which provides a key to the city's urbane humanism—the relationship between the individual and the mass. The very definition of any city traditionally includes its being a "mass container." Without the concentration of large numbers of people, there is no city (it would be well to remember that this large concentration in itself does not guarantee that there *will be* a city). It is not simply a question of mathematical definitions; concentration of population in a true urban container leads to a qualitative, not simply a quantitative, difference in life. The multiplying of the possibilities of accidental encounters, the excitation of personal ambitions confronted by such large potential audiences, the simultaneous feelings of isolation-in-mass and yet of urban solidarity-in-mass, the concentration of culture possible both technically and financially due to a concentration of population—all these factors make for a difference in the very quality of life as well as its accidental quantities. But given the basic need for large urban masses of people as part of the definition of any city, a new problem arises, a problem unknown to countryside or village. This is the problem of how an individual may relate himself to the crowds around him, and how they may relate themselves to him. The relationship in itself is central to any possible judgment of the success or failure of any given urban civilization.

In very many modern cities, ranging from London to Tokyo, from Chicago to Moscow, it has come to be assumed that individuals are deprived of their identity, their dignity and their human solidarity by being compressed into the urban mass. The "lonely crowd" has come to seem a permanent definition of urban life. And if the mass destroys the individual, it is assumed also that the mass itself, definable by and appealable to its lowest common denominator, is the enemy of all culture, all progress. It is to be manipulated for commercial or political reasons, managed for its own good (or bad), destroyed in war, above all contained, held at bay. The impersonality of architecture and of city planning in so many cities is simply an expression of this attitude. And such impersonally created environments in turn reinforce the individual's self-contempt and the crowd's smoldering dissatisfaction.

What, for example, can be the effect on individual human beings of being surrounded every minute of their lives by colossal gray- or stone- or steel-colored skyscrapers? The existence of such monuments to commercial greed or political power is a daily reminder to all who see them of their own insignificance, of their personal helplessness and isolation in the face of corporate or collective power. And what in turn is the effect of such personal feelings of inadequacy upon large groups of people? The personal feeling of impotence is often expressed, we are told by psychologists, in hysterical outbursts of rage punctuating long periods of depressed anxiety. The recent history of very many cities, illustrated by riots of all kinds, a flight from law and order and the final explosion of wars, would seem to indicate that the psychology of the mass reflects the psychology of the individual— magnified a thousandfold.

The history of Barcelona, in many respects more riotous and violent than that of most other Western cities, certainly reflects the nineteenth and early twentieth century breakdown of social cohesion and order brought about by the rise of competitive, money-oriented, production-dominated social and economic factors in urban life. But due to perhaps fortuitous factors, the forces of civic destruction never quite erased older, more humane values and attitudes to life in Barcelona. And with the close of the paleotechnic phase of economic development, the healing over of older social wounds and simple exhaustion, perhaps, these surviving values have had, as we have seen, a chance to reassert themselves.

The dignity and eccentricity of the individual is very highly respected in Barcelona. It is based on individual self-respect. Witness the marked absence of beggars on Barcelona streets during even the worst days following the civil and Second World wars. Witness the theoretical fact that a man placed under arrest in Barcelona, should he resist arrest sufficiently, is not to be beaten, mobbed or manhandled by the police. He may, however, be shot dead. Two rather perverse examples—but important. It is assumed that, given a final choice, a man aware of the consequences of his actions is himself responsible for them. He is not to be subjected to physical indignities, but, if he so chooses, may suffer a final penalty. Of course, in practice, Barcelona policemen (that is to say, the Guardia Civil, which is generally called upon at times of real disorder) do not go about shooting people. And during, for example, student riots, they employ many of the same means of crowd control seen in New York, London or Tokyo—the fire hoses, the horses, the night-stick-swinging charges. But in theory and in law the other alternative is open to both sides. On occasion it is chosen. It is assumed that a man means what he does, means what he says, and means it sufficiently to suffer whatever consequences may be involved in his action.

And, too, there are and have been beggars in the city. But their attitude has traditionally been one of dignity and self-possession. They do not assume that a passing stranger owes them anything. They assume only that a fellow man, recognizing their individual dignity, will respond if able to individual need.

This self-valuation is evident in the self-respect of those who perform the city's most menial work. Street

*Amid a maze of medieval street patterns,*
*a policeman is often more efficient than traffic lights—*
*and more responsive to traffic emergencies.*

sweepers, cleaning women, the old men who supervise the parking of cars on certain streets (they will watch them for you while you are absent and, since none of them have ever driven a car, elegantly direct you into collision with the nearest tree, parked car, or the curb), all display a consciousness of the value of their work—a value lent to it by the simple fact that they are performing it— which transcends economic motivations or social classifications.

It may be said that these are national, not necessarily civic, characteristics. The Spaniard anywhere in his country partakes to greater or lesser extent of a noble heritage, a tragic sense of life, fatalism and the basic assumptions of Christian doctrine (the most important, in the present instance, being that every man has a soul and hence an innate worth utterly irrespective of his social, economic or political condition). This is true, and yet Barcelona has preserved these values within the urban container—and in turn, the very structure of the city reflects them.

There are no supercolossal buildings in Barcelona to dwarf the onlooker. There are no throughways to frighten him into recognition of his fragility in a machine world. There is no feeling of giantism about any of his environment. And because of the survival of local influences in his life, generally expressed through local ritual, the individual can relate himself in meaningful ways with his neighbors. He is not isolated unless he chooses to be (and it is difficult to make that choice in Barcelona). There is no "lonely crowd" in the city.

Ritual, the uses of time and the self-valuation of the citizen as a citizen come together in and are very well expressed by the *sardana,* the Catalan national dance, which is danced on any and every occasion, by one and all, in any appropriate place. The *sardana* is so old that no two authorities will agree on its origins: it is older than the Gothic Quarter, perhaps older than the Roman foundations of the city. Its form is that of a linked circle, its music a two-step, its atmosphere one of real consecration. The participants (as many can join the circle as wish) maintain very composed, almost severe, expressions on their faces as they go through the graceful steps; even the children. Despite its great antiquity, there is nothing folkloric about it— no costumes (people dance it in whatever clothes they happen to be wearing), no self-conscious atmosphere of participating in a performance. It is, despite its rigid form, a very current, modern expression, appearing as natural to the city as the oldest or the newest buildings in it. Dancers and spectators (there are always more dancers than spectators) are deeply aware that in dancing the *sardana* they are asserting Catalan culture, Catalan apartness. But they are also asserting (and aware of it) a broad civic identity, a celebration of the fact that they are citizens of Barcelona. They are testifying to continuity with those who have gone before; bearing witness to the past, to the future and to themselves as part of a great and continuing community; they are affirming that in some respects at least they have kept faith with their predecessors, that the essential communal civic spirit of the city and its humane values still survive.

To generalize about nearly two million people, to try to reduce to words attitudes and ways of life which are not measurable in statistical analyses, is, of course,

*The* sardana—*public affirmation of individual dignity, collective responsibility in a continuing civic order* always dangerous. Life in Barcelona, as elsewhere, is fluid—one can offer only a snapshot, a still photograph, of what is really a fast-moving kaleidoscope. Nevertheless the three aspects of urban life we have isolated in Barcelona are very real. They are the fruit of the structure of the city, and they influence that structure mightily. Assuming that humane values are worth preserving, can Barcelona and its people withstand the new pressures which have extinguished such values elsewhere?

# 7 Enter a Few Villains

*These thousands of people who hurry under
pressure along the sidewalks will maintain their
way of life, their Mediterranean manners ...*

—FEDERICO UDINA

Perhaps. But some of the real villains of modern urban
life have only recently arrived onstage in Barcelona.
It remains to be seen whether they can be resisted,
banished or perhaps charmed out of existence or at
least staved off until solutions can be found.

The villains are easily identifiable to citizens of
other cities. The New Yorker would immediately point
out the burgeoning traffic problems; the Londoner
would recognize the familiar smog that afflicts his own
city; the Chicagoan would understand the problems
of a city gobbling up countryside in every direction;
the Angeleno would note with alarm the increasing
pressure to slice up the city with throughways for the
benefit of motorists; the Parisian would shudder

sympathetically at the veritable flood of tourists inundating the city and its facilities. All of them would, perhaps, see the outlines of modern economic and social demands which have all but destroyed urbanity in each of their home cities.

The most identifiable villains are linked together—traffic and smog. Over the past ten years the number of cars and trucks using the streets and avenues has increased more dramatically in Barcelona than in any other city in the world—largely because until recently there were but few to be seen. Until a few years after the Second World War, Spain produced no cheap motor vehicles (the handmade Pegaso was a luxury sports car). Furthermore, partly as a means of raising revenue, partly because the country had neither the roads nor the garage facilities to accommodate them, import taxes on foreign manufactured vehicles were fantastically high. Only the rich could afford cars. But since the Second World War Spain has permitted the manufacture under license (the Seat, built by Italian-owned Fiat; the Dodge Dart; Land Rover and others) of cars in Spain. Excise taxes make them more than twice as expensive as similar models manufactured outside the country, and import taxes remain a staggering 120 per cent. But the wave of prosperity that has washed over Spain in the last decade has distributed enough money to enough people to provide a mass market for automobiles even at these terribly inflated prices.

In 1961 there were but 123,000 motor vehicles of all descriptions in Barcelona. By 1965 there were more than 240,000. The best estimate for today is nearly half a million! Half a million vehicles—for a city of less

*Underground parking ramps in the Plaza Cataluña—
the final admission that traffic has triumphed
over more human uses of this great open space.*

than one and a half million residents. At the present rate there will soon be far more vehicles than citizens on Barcelona's streets. Most of the increase has been in privately operated automobiles. And if the private car has proved the mortal enemy of cities all over the world, it is especially deadly in Barcelona because of that city's particular history.

Traffic jams, with their nerve-rending confusion and noise, their poisonous fumes and their threat to life are bad enough in cities such as New York, where the streets and avenues were designed to accommodate wheeled traffic. But in Barcelona, where most of the central city, especially the Gothic Quarter, preserves a layout intended to accommodate pedestrians or, at most, small animal-drawn carts, traffic snarls and jams can be positively frightening. It doesn't matter that most of the cars are much smaller than American automobiles; Barcelona's central streets are simply not designed to handle motor traffic of any kind. But most business is done in the central city, and it is the businessmen who, above all others, can afford cars. Furthermore, most commerce is located in the central city and requires deliveries and shipments by truck. Industry, with its fantastic traffic demands, came late to Barcelona and is concentrated outside the central city—with roads partially adequate for its needs; but industrial truck shipments across the city have added this heavy load, too, to the general traffic nightmare.

Parking is all but impossible in downtown Barcelona. The streets are generally too narrow to accommodate a lane of parked cars as well as even a one-way lane of traffic. Land occupied by old buildings is too valuable to turn into parking lots. Parking garages, which would have to displace commercial enterprises or historic buildings, cannot be provided. So the owner of a car who drives to work in Barcelona is faced with terrible circulation problems and the final frustration of having no place to dispose of his vehicle. But it is not the woes of motorists that are of primary concern here, it is the damage that motor vehicles have inflicted on the city as a whole.

Take for an example the broad Plaza Cataluña. It is ringed by a wide circular road that connects the most important traffic arteries of the city—the Ramblas, the Via Layetana, the Paseo de Gracia among others. It has become an infernal whirlpool of thousands of desperate motorists careening around its central gardens, trying to escape into one of the main streets. Pedestrian underpasses have been built. But who wants to scuttle under the street to the gardens and fountains in the center, only to find himself surrounded by a smelly, noisy, nerve-wracking continuous traffic jam? In effect, the Plaza Cataluña has been ruined as a resting, strolling or meeting place. Even its famous pigeons have begun to flee its dangerous precincts.

And Plaza Cataluña, it will be recalled, was built relatively recently and was criticized as being beyond the human scale. When the same sort of traffic invasion hits the older, smaller plazas in which Barcelona abounds, the results are much worse. And even when a plaza does not become a whirlpool of internal combustion engines, its use simply as a parking area does much to destroy its essential beauty and usefulness. For example, the Plaza Real, off the Ramblas, is a marvelously preserved model of late Renaissance architecture and planning—quiet, peaceful, beautiful with its fountain and gardens, the resort of strollers, sitters, stamp collectors (on Sundays). It has but one traffic entrance, hence there is little motor movement within it. But it is such a convenient parking place adjacent to the central Ramblas that its four sides are lined with cars—and the beauty and symmetry of the plaza is thereby destroyed. Traffic has also been allowed to invade certain fringe areas of the Gothic Quarter with disastrous aesthetic results.

If traffic flow and parking can destroy the quality and usefulness of plazas, they can do the same to streets and avenues. When traffic is permitted to flow down the narrow streets of the Gothic Quarter or the Chinese Quarter, it makes those streets a death trap for pedestrians. But even the relatively wider Ramblas (two lanes on either side of the central mall) cannot maintain its character against the traffic onslaught. People strolling down the beautiful central mall, or shopping along it for birds and flowers and books, or sitting on its benches to rest, find themselves in the middle of an arterial maelstrom.

And in Barcelona particularly, traffic threatens the very fabric of social life by ruining the outdoor café. To sit outside at a café table, chatting with friends or whiling away the time, becomes all but impossible when cars and trucks and motorbikes are roaring and fuming past within five feet of one's eyes, ears and nose. Yet the presence of hundreds of outdoor cafés right in the middle of the central city, on its streets and plazas, where they are most needed as an antidote to the world of business and commerce, is one of the essential distinctions of Barcelona as a place to live and of the way of life of its citizens.

And traffic poses other, more subtle but no less dangerous problems. In its modern districts and districts-in-the-making Barcelona has succeeded better than most cities in creating and re-creating itself as a work of art. This, as we have seen, has been based on the citizen's appreciation of inherited art forms from the past and his insistence on the continuance of that consciously decorative tradition. Buildings one can sit and admire or regard with interest while walking past have a built-in protection against demolition in the personal fondness with which they are regarded by very many people. New buildings are likewise subject to a critical scrutiny by the public and are measured against past standards. But when people can no longer sit and look at a building, or walk by it—when they speed past it in a car—then no building undergoes either the examination it deserves or the development of personal attachment. A basis of protection for older buildings, and critical standards for new, is removed.

Traffic also splits neighborhoods. As the city attempts to cope with its mounting motorized congestion, some streets become one-way, others are banned to cars. Motorists, seeking the fastest route to their destination, begin to use side streets, thereby converting formerly peaceful neighborhoods into traffic thoroughfares and effectively destroying their primary functions as local meeting places, playgrounds and connecting links in the complex and subtle web of community relationships. This is an assault on another

*The vital, human use of open space expressed triumphantly every Sunday by the stamp collectors of Plaza Real.*

central aspect of Barcelona life—the traditional *local* identification of its citizens.

And, finally, by increasing the speed of movement, the motorcar increases the pace of life. Punctuality, time compulsion, nervous disorders, indigestion, the tensions that destroy human sensibilities—all may come to mark life in Barcelona if ever its pace is speeded to the frenzy of such cities as New York or Paris.

Traffic makes its contribution, too, to Barcelona's smog problem. Like all industrial cities, Barcelona is poisoning its atmosphere daily with the discharge from hundreds of factory smokestacks. But because these are mostly on the city's outskirts, combined with the fact that Barcelona is backed by mountains (which raise air masses flowing over them) and fronts on the sea, smog, in the past, has been a relatively small nuisance. But the influx of motor vehicles is now changing all that. Gasoline is as expensive in Spain as it is elsewhere in Europe (about double the American price). So despite the smaller cubic capacity of Spanish-European internal combustion cylinders, driving vehicles for profit almost requires that they be propelled by the much cheaper diesel fuel. There are about 7,000 taxis, 1,000 buses, and perhaps 60,000 trucks in Barcelona, and economics dictates that they be constructed with diesel engines and consume diesel oil. But although the resulting exhaust has been found to be less poisonous than that of gasoline, its stench is intolerable. The entire city now hides beneath a gray-brown cloud of diesel exhaust and the awful smell of diesel fumes is prevalent along every main thorough-

*The motorcycle truck—the new burro
of Spain—ingenious answer
to narrow streets, expensive gasoline*

fare and street. It has become as noticeable and distinct and particular to Barcelona as is fog to London
or San Francisco. And this odor is another assault
against the outdoor life of the city.

Related to the traffic problem (though not yet its
principal cause, which remains local automobile use)
is the fact that Barcelona is the main route and funnel
for motoring tourists entering Spain. Only a hundred

miles from the French frontier, the city sits at the end of the only throughway linking the Mediterranean coasts of France and Spain. Tourists driving their own cars and those brought down by bus *must* pass through Barcelona to reach the southern Spanish coast or the Balearic Islands.

It has been suggested that the throughway be extended to slice through the city; that it be circled around to bypass the city; that it tunnel under the city. None of these solutions is particularly attractive. But when it is remembered that some 20,000,000 tourists per year descend upon Spain and that perhaps 4,000,000 of them enter by motorcar or coach on the Barcelona route, it will be seen that some solution must be effected. At present the cars and buses flowing down the throughway from the French frontier are led into the city by an irrational and complicated series of city avenues and streets, to lose themselves among the city's own congested arteries and contribute to local traffic snarls.

Tunneling under the city would involve an expenditure entirely too great for the tax structure to bear; bypassing the city is complicated by the engineering problems of leading a throughway through the mountains that all but enclose the approaches from the north. There remains the most obvious solution—the conversion of a series of avenues into a throughway slicing right through the city. But the experience of other cities, especially Los Angeles, is well known in Barcelona. The urban devastation that space-eating throughways can inflict on a city is second only to the urban devastation caused by war. It is very much to the credit of the planning consciousness and civic responsibility of the municipal authorities that, despite the engineering problems (which will involve a series of tunnels through certain hills and mountains) and the resulting higher taxes that must be imposed to pay for it, the bypass solution is the one that has been chosen. But even this will inflict some harm, because since Barcelona now meets its northern and northwestern fringe of hills and mountains, the bypass throughway will have to cut through the newer sections of the city anyhow. But at least it is being planned for and it will not disturb the old core or the central city.

The problems of expansion, of urban giantism, came to Barcelona late enough to be recognized but too late to prevent some of its problems. As in other cities, the problem is based on the exodus from the central city of people who prefer to live in more countrified surroundings and can afford to travel to and from the central city for work or play. This is the problem which has destroyed the countryside surrounding such cities as New York and London and ringed them with vast, impersonal, dormitory suburbs where the population finds no civic focus, no sense of allegiance to a community and no feelings of responsibility for a civic or social order. It is also at the root of the traffic and parking problems that damage the central city because of daily commuting.

From the viewpoint of the countryside itself, the outward spread of the city is an encroachment on the physical as well as the moral and social environment. And when Barcelona gobbled up the towns of San Gervasio and Sarria and others less than fifty years ago, these towns quickly lost their civic identity, even if the architects and planners were careful to preserve their ancient cores. People generally live in small towns because they prefer to. When they find themselves suddenly transposed into an urban situation, cannibalized as it were, they are as lost as is the city dweller suddenly dumped into the countryside. They find their small town being swamped by new residential building, invaded by a huge number of people who owe it no particular allegiance and who will use it only as a dormitory—a sleeping area from whence they sally daily into the central city. The customs, traditions and atmosphere of the town are destroyed, and they are not, or at least not immediately, replaced by the customs and traditions of the city. The environment, in other words, is destroyed for what it was and not soon restructured.

If the invasion of the countryside and the gobbling up of small towns is hard on those who dwell there, it brings new problems to the invading city. Here now are many thousands of people, an increasing proportion of the city's population (in New York and London, the overwhelming majority) who live remote enough from the central city so that it becomes to them only a place to work, not to live or play (except for the irregular dash in to see a play or listen to a concert). Such people now see the city only as a place to exploit for their own economic advantage. They resent paying taxes to improve central-city areas, and they demand that central-city streets be made into commuting thoroughfares and that central-city areas be made into parking lots. Having fled the urban environment, they then turn on it to destroy it.

Barcelona is not one of the world's largest cities, but it is one of the world's most rapidly expanding

*The Plaza del Pino—what can happen
to public open space when it is turned
over to vehicles.*

medium-sized cities. And the expansion is *now*. The older villages swallowed up by the outward push of the years before the civil war were still close enough to the heart of the city to be urbanized in the process. They did not become suburbs but rather new districts of the city. The problems of incorporating them were architectural and, as we have seen, brilliantly solved. But the new expansion is into areas remote enough from the central city to be considered suburbs, if such a condition is allowed to befall them. Public transportation to and from and between these new outlying areas is scanty. They are beyond the subway lines, serviced only by bus routes. But the cost of fuel and the spread-out nature of the region involved makes the provision of rapid transit all but economically impossible there. So Barcelona's expansion is based on the private motorcar—with all that implies in damage to the central city.

West and southwest of the city, along the highways to Saragossa and to Valencia, little enclaves of private or semiprivate houses are springing up. They could almost be modernistic country villages except that they have no civic core or possibilities. They are only places for people to sleep (from which the men fight their way through traffic to work while the women grow bored with the aimless life of a suburb which is neither city nor country). It is not hard to foresee the time when such little developments, spreading and linking up, can form the same kind of dreary suburban belt around Barcelona as is today to be found around Chicago, Paris, Berlin and Denver. New and beautifully designed public schools are going up in these areas to accommodate the children, while the much more

heavily attended central-city schools remain, in too
many cases, dilapidated and overcrowded. New roads
bisecting these areas are broad, well paved, well able
to handle the traffic which they will then pour into
the smaller, ever more congested central city streets
and avenues. Almost all these new houses have built-
in garages to accommodate the urbanity-devouring ma-
chines they daily loose upon the city. So far the new
suburban areas are small and scattered but their
threat is implicit. The small towns beyond them have
already the air of enterprises going out of business,
waiting resignedly and glumly to be transformed not
into an urban pattern, which however painful the
process, might instill urban excitement into their
ways of life, but waiting rather to be transformed into
dormitory suburbs, engulfed in the pallid fog of suburban boredom, their country-town vitality drained,
urban vitality denied them.

These areas, with their implicit threat of giantism,
are beyond the range of the Provincial Council urbanization plan, beyond the range of even the garden-city
zones. The Provincial Council has all necessary authority to incorporate them into its planning—in fact it has
authority to plan the entire province around Barcelona. But such authority, exerted in the face of pre-
existing patterns, may prove insufficient to prevent
suburbia. What the council permits today beyond the
range of its zoning laws, it may find extremely difficult
to change tomorrow. But the question is, Will the
council, the municipal authorities, the people of Barcelona want to carry on their age-old urban life tomorrow? The pressures against it are growing daily—
they are the same pressures which have brought about

the first signs of urban and civic distintegration and disorder, whose symptoms are traffic snarls, smog, the big speed-up and giantism.

The basic question remains, What is Barcelona meant to be? In most other cities the question has been answered—an environment to exploit for profit. This attitude is a direct outgrowth and intensification of the basic attitude of Western capitalist-industrialist civilization. The earth and all things on it and in it exist to be exploited for the profit of the individual, or a certain group of individuals. In some cities, such as London, this attitude is restrained and modified by an ancient tradition of civic spirit based on older (medieval) social forms. In others it may be modified by state-imposed restrictions (one thinks of Leningrad, Budapest). In still others it is hardly modified at all (New York, Paris, Chicago). If the city, any city, is looked upon as an environment strictly for exploitation, then that city is doomed as a city. It may survive as a gigantic commercial enterprise, accommodating the residence of transient businessmen or workers (Manhattan seems headed for this category), or as a center devoted almost entirely to industrial production, housing only the industrial workers and the engineers and managers (Pittsburgh has long since become such a city)—but as a city, as a place to celebrate the human experience, to create, preserve and transmit a human culture, such huge centers will not survive.

The vital question has come late to Barcelona for a

*Preservation of the Gothic Stage on the intimate level of the entrance courtyard of a private building*

variety of reasons, some of them determined by past history, others as accidental as anything in human history can be. There is, first of all, the survival of the Catholic religious tradition in Barcelona in a very real, as opposed to a merely formal, sense. This is important not only for its contribution to a sense of ritual and continuity in urban life, but also because, despite the gradual diminishing of the faith among the citizens of Barcelona, despite the avowed atheism of many and the indifference of nearly all to the strictly theological and clerical aspects of religion, the Catholic tradition continues to uphold, for all citizens to see, the idea of another order of life, another way of being, besides the current commercial materialism. By being born into this tradition, and raised in it, and constantly reminded of it, no matter how vigorously the people of Barcelona may consciously reject it in many of its forms, they have been imbued with a knowledge of the Christian ideal—not a competitive ideal but a socially responsible ideal. They can never forget that the very structure of their city was once ordered upon a mundane imitation of the City of God, and that precisely during those medieval centuries Barcelona achieved its greatest wealth, power and civic glory. Since there was no Reformation in Spain and the Church has maintained itself there as an influence on political, social and economic life to a far greater extent than in other countries, the civic ideals of Christianity have also survived as a constant brake upon the ruthlessly exploitive view of human life and nature.

Secondly, capitalist organization may have come early to Barcelona, but its worst expression in early industrialism came very late—more than one hundred years after it came, for example, to England. It came late enough so that those most bitterly exploited by it, the workers, had already been to a certain extent instructed and imbued with theoretical means of resistance to it. This resistance created nearly a century of unrest and civic strife culminating in a bloody civil war; although the traditionalists won that war in the end, their victory was conditioned by the realization that they could never finally feel secure in the enjoyment of it without substantial concessions to progressive ideas and democratic ways, in reality if not in form. This led to two things. First of all, as a part of a continuing opposition deprived of other forms of expression, the poorer people of Barcelona have clung to old rituals, a feeling of localism which they see also as a means of defiance (however indirect) against the imposition of social conformity which in turn is essential to successful exploitation of human beings by other human beings. Secondly, it has caused the ruling classes in Barcelona to proceed with the utmost caution in any attempt to exploit the city, or even areas of it, for private profit.

A third factor has been the continuing tradition of Catalan (and Barcelona's) apartness from the rest of Spain. This has, as we have seen, very real economic, social and cultural foundations. But since the question of Catalonian independence has been settled (several times over) by force of arms, it can now only find expression through the preservation of older cultural forms and ideals—among these, the ideal of the city as a communion of all its people, which flourished when Catalonia was independent and great. And it also provides pressures making for unity between classes in

Barcelona, since all of them oppose centralized domination by the Spanish state.

These are the primary factors which have held in abeyance until our own time the spread and domination of exploitive views of the city. A system of historical and accidental "checks and balances" which has preserved older forms of civic behavior and postponed until now the dire question of whether Barcelona will continue to be an environment designed for human happiness and pleasure or whether it will, as have so many other cities, capitulate before images of wealth and power and become an environment for exploitation. The question can no longer be postponed. And to answer it, the real villains of modern society have made their appearance upon this historic civic stage.

Religious forms and influence, preserved until now, are facing disintegration. In the face of modern technology, science and power, the Christian idea of man's life on earth can survive no more in Barcelona than it does in New York or Kansas City. The erosion of religious faith, which in Barcelona has occurred principally only in the last seventy-five years, now threatens to undermine its surviving civic expressions. Ritual based on religious tradition is coming more and more to seem simply irrelevant to daily life. It is preserved now as an excuse for frivolity or as a money-making

*Older (nineteenth century) factories, such as this one on Calle Marques del Duero, came too late to really dominate the city—though they contribute their share to air pollution.*

scheme for local merchants or as a lure for tourists. But it is questionable if the forms of ritual can survive when their basic content has vanished. And ritual is not only an expression of the dignity of an individual or a group, it is also the rehearsal of that older ideal of the Christian metropolis, and is intimately bound up with the preservation of "locality" and neighborliness and the feeling of belonging which until now the citizen of Barcelona has enjoyed.

The economic and civic "stand-off" between those eager to exploit the city for their profit and those who have seen in the city's preservation their principal means of protecting themselves personally against exploitation is coming to an end, too. Of all the many statistics available on Spanish life, the one which reveals the amazing growth of the economy (double that of the American economy) is the most important. Early industrialism is a thing of the past in Barcelona. The new industries growing now around the city's outskirts are, like their counterparts in other lands, huge, utterly modern in design and operation and based on a tremendous concentration of wealth. They demand markets. They demand technical proficiency of a high order on the part of their employees as well as their managers. Markets mean advertising, mean the creation of a desire for material goods, mean the creation of a consumer-oriented society. This, in turn, implies new civic values; if the object of life is personal comfort, private acquisition, then every environment is exploitable to that end. Technical proficiency implies punctuality, order, an educational emphasis on the virtues of discipline. It demands the destruction and clearing away of the old (whether ideas or buildings) in the interests of efficiency. The reward for all this is a higher material standard of living; its price (as the inhabitants of Boston, Moscow, Tokyo and Sydney now know all too well) is the dehumanizing of life.

And Catalan apartness, the sense of Barcelona's civic independence which has preserved so many human cultural forms and activities in the city's life, and which has also led so many Catalan men of ability to seek careers on the civic rather than the national stage, is also vanishing. The modern industrialization of Barcelona and the entire Catalan province has made archaic any idea of Catalonian independence. The Catalan economy is now intricately enmeshed with that of the rest of Spain. Although still cherishing their sense of cultural difference, most citizens of Barcelona now realize that geographically, economically, historically and, increasingly, socially they are and must remain part of the Spanish national state. And where modern technology produces so great a pressure for conformity, can cultural distinctions long survive?

The practical results of all this are becoming daily more evident in Barcelona. There is the increasing crime rate, and the increasing rate, especially of aimless antisocial crime, of the sort of juvenile delinquency with which American cities have long been familiar. There is the failure to cope with traffic problems—important not only on its many practical levels but also as a symptom of the fact that the people of the city care less about their environment than they have in the past. There is the vastly increased pace of life (noticeable over the span of only ten years) and

*In a bar, the haphazard, the immediate, the intimately personal make for a more humane atmosphere.*

the new enterprises devoted to serving it—the self-service shops, the scattering of supermarkets, the sprouting of cafeterias and snack bars in place of restaurants. There is the increasing cynicism with which the people of the city view the old rituals that once expressed their civic involvement. And much, much more.

But, as we have pointed out, these villains have only recently appeared. Despite the ravages they have already wrought, enough of the form and content of an older, more humane view of life and the urban environment remains to dispute possession of the civic stage. The future is not necessarily a forgone conclusion in Barcelona—not yet. The forces of modern technological integration and social organization threaten a still-preserved humane way of life in Barcelona, but they have not yet won. Barcelona still has a choice.

EPILOGUE: # Finale or Curtain Raiser?

*And although the things that happened to me there
were not very pleasant, if not actually wearisome,
still I bore them without a grudge just for the
pleasure of having seen the place.*

—DON QUIXOTE DE LA MANCHA

(MIGUEL DE CERVANTES)

If Don Quixote's verdict on the city of Barcelona seems
a bit somber (his words could almost have been pro-
nounced by some traffic-stranded tourist of today), it
would be well to remember that the estimable knight
was always getting himself into trouble no matter
where he was. But his troubles were, after all, strictly
human foibles; he was the victim of himself rather
than of his environment. And so long as the troubles
of the people of Barcelona can be kept to the human
scale, they can continue to bear them without a grudge.
The threat, of course, is that their troubles will soon
pass beyond the human dimension into that area of
statistical mass dissatisfaction and discontent which
has all but ended meaningful urban life elsewhere. The

human drama still being performed on Barcelona's civic stage may be coming to an end, to be replaced by the pointless and dreary round of frenzied exploitation which passes for urbanity in other cities. Or it may not. Before speculating about the future, it would be well to ask ourselves a few questions.

First of all, Who cares? Can it matter to other people in other cities whether or not the people of Barcelona can maintain a humane way of life in a modern urban environment? Yes, it can matter vitally. It would be pointless, for example, to establish the fact that the citizens of, say, Florence, Italy, or Sacramento, California, enjoy a more satisfactory, more intimate and more humane way of life than do the citizens of Leeds, England, or Denver, Colorado, or Birmingham, Alabama. Of course they do. But neither Florence nor Sacramento are facing the terribly urgent and intense pressures of modern industrialization. Barcelona, on the other hand, in size, complexity, industry and "modernity" faces problems of a very meaningful nature. Their solution (or the failure to find a solution) can be of tremendous interest to city planners, civic administrators and just plain urban citizens throughout the world. If a humane way of life can be maintained in Barcelona, it can be maintained elsewhere—and where it does not yet exist it may even be created. Just as individuals may influence others simply by "bearing witness" to a truth, so cities may do the same.

Secondly, what about the peculiar and fortunate circumstances of Barcelona's preservation of the past? There is no Gothic Quarter to be found in any American city (very few, for that matter, in European cities). How can one expect the citizens of cities with much

shorter histories to duplicate the sense of civic continuity, the attitude of preserving the city as a work of
art? Civic wisdom and public taste cannot be created
by decree or even be voted into existence; they can
only grow over very long periods of time. True, but
they cannot even begin to grow unless citizens have a
common objective, that objective being the creation or
re-creation of their environment as a place for human
enjoyment and human development. The fact that the
people of Barcelona live much more pleasant, relaxed
and personally fruitful lives than the people of most
other large cities continues to provide an example and
a goal. It cannot forever be kept secret from the people of other cities that the price of urbanity is not necessarily endless war against their environment, that
in the world of modern technology their standard of
living does not necessarily demand a life of haste, tension and ugliness. So long as the people of Barcelona
can achieve the same material success as people in
other cities without sacrificing either themselves or
their environment, they once again "bear witness" to
the possibilities of urban life and give other citizens
of other cities a meaningful goal. One need not be inspired by the past to demand a decent environment in
the present—that others enjoy it is sufficient goad.

But both the physical and human environment of
Barcelona is the result of a long, particular and national, perhaps racial, development as much as it is the
result of purely civic influences? True again, but men

*One of the most superb urban open places in the world—the
small, but exquisitely proportioned Plaza Real. This is the city
as human environment.*

are free to make their own history—freer today than ever before. And it is not expected that if the millennium arrived tomorrow and the citizens of Chicago suddenly began to enjoy a humane life amid pleasant urban surroundings that life would take the same form or find the same means of expression that it does in Barcelona. But every national culture has within it resources from which a meaningful and humane life can be created and with which it can be celebrated—if only the people set that as their goal. Most cities in the modern world have become shrines to naked power, either the power of commerce (New York, Chicago, Marseilles, Nagasaki) or the power of the state (Washington, Moscow, Paris, Brasília). And apologists for this condition have insisted that since an acceptable standard of living is the result of a concentration of economic and political power, the worship of power is, if regrettable, inevitable. But power (both economic and political) is concentrated as meaningfully in Barcelona as in any city of comparable size anywhere in the world—and it is *not* worshiped—and the standard of living remains very high. Again, Barcelona proves that it is possible for a modern industrial-commercial city of great size to remain a shrine to humanity and its culture, rather than to power.

But modern social and economic pressures—the "villains" on the urban stage—have only recently made their appearance in Barcelona, and it remains to be seen whether or not a humane life can be maintained

*The central mall of the Ramblas (Lyceo Theater in background) converts the city's busiest thoroughfare into its most popular strolling area.*

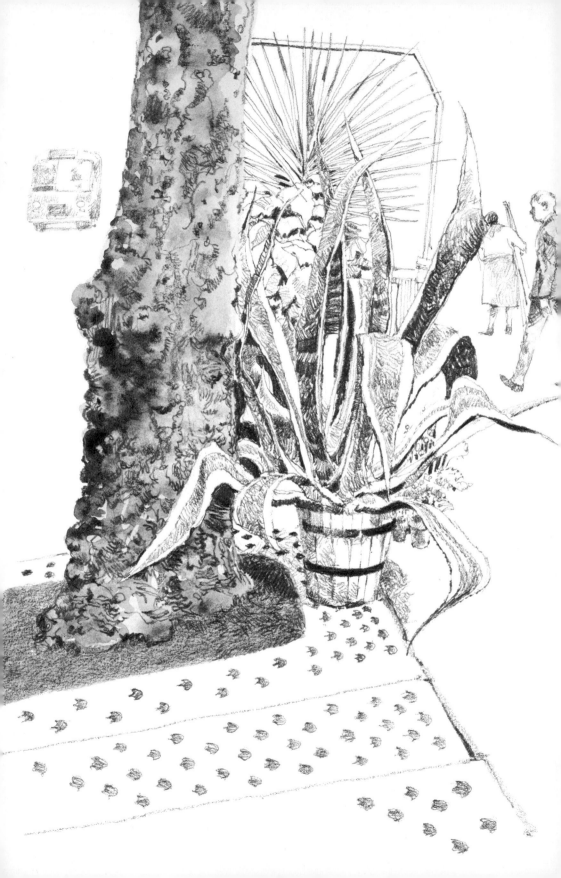

in their presence. True—and the crisis point is precisely *now*. On the Barcelona stage, we are witnessing either the finale of the last act of its great urban drama, or the opening of a new and hardly predictable life-play.

If the new symptoms of social disintegration and civic fragmentation—the traffic, the smog, the increasing pace of life, the cynicism undermining old rituals, the giantism that is beginning to afflict the city—give grounds for pessimism about the future, there are certain new factors which may be cause for hope. First and foremost among these is self-consciousness. The people and the municipal and provincial governments of Barcelona are very keenly aware of the urban problems growing up around them. Since the problems have arrived late, they are able to benefit from the good or, more frequently, bad experiences of other cities. And they do benefit energetically. If, for example, the city planners of Barcelona had not had the horrid evidence from other places of what cutting throughways across a city can do, they might have been tempted to choose this drastic solution to the problem of tourist traffic moving down from France. Without the example of suburbia from Long Island to London, perhaps the Provincial Council of Barcelona might have permitted the establishment of suburban patterns of development around the city. Without the example of the inhuman impact of Manhattan's skyscrapers, perhaps Barcelona today would boast such

*The flower stalls along the Ramblas—portable civic gardens for the pedestrian make strolling a delight.*

symbols of naked power. Above all, without the example of other cities throughout the world which have allowed themselves to become environments for private exploitation, perhaps Barcelona's people and civic leaders would have permitted the uncontrolled and haphazard development of their city. But they have fallen into none of these traps as yet. And awareness of them may be more than half the battle.

It is not possible at the present time to predict Barcelona's future. Its geography assures that the city will continue to exist and also to grow physically (unless, of course, other men in other cities lose control of themselves and their cataclysmic weapons). Whether it will continue as a human environment or become simply another center of self-exploitation, cannot yet be foreseen. (The very fact that it cannot be foreseen may be taken as a sign of hope.) If the humane urban drama comes to a close in Barcelona, then that city, like the older Gothic Quarter which is still its heart, will simply bear witness to an urban way of life that once was and might have been. But if a modern urban drama is only now opening on the civic stage of Barcelona, then that city may become an example and an inspiration to cities throughout the world—may contain in its very being some of the seeds of a new flowering of a truly humane, truly worldwide, urban culture.

*¡ Viva Barcelona !*

# Index

# Index

Turkey, 31

Udina, Federico, 158
Unamuno, Miguel de, 134
Usatges, 25, 34
utilities, public, 10, 12, 94, 96–
97

Via Layetana, 72, 162
Victorian section, 53, 69

Vikings, 47
Visigoths, 19–20, 22

War of the Segadores, 34–35
Wars of the Spanish Succession, 35
Wellesley, Sir Arthur, 39
World War II, 60, 96, 113, 124, 126, 152, 159
Wright, Frank Lloyd, 113